D0895637

VOLUME 11 OF 14 VOLUMES

THE LINCOLN LIBRARY OF SPORTS CHAMPIONS

SEVENTH EDITION

Cleveland, Ohio

The Lincoln Library of Sports Champions, Seventh Edition

For more information contact: The Lincoln Library Press, 812 Huron Road E Ste 401, Cleveland, Ohio 44115–1172. Or visit our web site at: www.TheLincolnLibrary.com

The Lincoln Library Press is an imprint of, and The Lincoln Library owl is a trademark of, Eastword Publications Development, Inc., Cleveland, Ohio.

Although every effort has been made to ensure the accuracy of the information contained herein, The Lincoln Library Press does not guarantee the accuracy of the data. Errors submitted to and verified by the publisher will be corrected in future editions.

Cataloging-in-Publication Data

The Lincoln library of sports champions. — 7th ed.
Cleveland, Ohio : Lincoln Library, c2004.
14 v.
Summary: Presents brief, alphabetically arranged biographies of 300 great sports personalities, past and present, from around the world. Some of the new sports included in this edition are women's hockey, wheelchair sports, and extreme sports. Features a table of contents arranged by sport, indexes by gender, nationality, and historic era plus a supplementary reading list.

ISBN 0–912168–19–6 (set)

1. Athletes—Biography—Encyclopedias, Juvenile.
[1. Athletes—Encyclopedias. 2. Sports—Encyclopedias.]
I. Gall, Timothy L.
GV697.A1 L56 2004
796.0922—dc22 2004-92275

Manufactured in Hong Kong

10 9 8 7 6 5 4 3 2 1

The Lincoln Library Press,
inspiring independent inquisitive minds,
is named for Abraham Lincoln,
America's foremost autodidact.

CONTENTS

Volume 11

Namath, Joe

Joe Namath (1943–) football player, was born in Beaver Falls, Pennsylvania. He began participating in athletics when he was young and was a star football, basketball, and baseball player in high school. Although he could have signed a major league baseball contract with the Chicago Cubs, Namath decided to attend the University of Alabama. At Alabama, he became one of the top college quarterbacks in the nation. Namath signed a contract with the New York Jets of the American Football League (AFL) after being drafted by them in the first round. He received Rookie-of-the-Year honors in 1965. In 1967, he set a record for yards gained passing in a season with 4007. The cocky, outspoken player led the Jets to the Super Bowl championship in

1969 and was selected the Most Valuable Player in the title game and the AFL Player (MVP) of the Year. Throughout his career, Namath was plagued by knee injuries. He played a year with the Los Angeles Rams before retiring in 1978. Joe Namath was inducted into the Pro Football Hall of Fame in 1985.

Pro football has been on the sports pages of newspapers throughout the country for a long time. Longhaired, free-wheeling Joe Namath also put pro ball on the front pages, the society pages, and the editorial pages. On the football field or off, "Broadway Joe" had a flair for drama and controversy.

His playing record had its ups and downs. Sometimes he was benched by his coaches. But Joe Namath had few equals when it came to making a key pass completion in a crucial game.

One of Namath's greatest games was against the Baltimore Colts in January 1969, in the Super Bowl. It was played in the Miami, Florida, Orange Bowl. Football forecasters had rated Namath's team, the Jets, a whopping 17-point underdog to the Baltimore Colts.

At a banquet a few days before

In 1967, Namath was the leading passer in the AFL with 4007 yards on 258 completions.

JETS
12

*As his teammates set to block,
Namath drops back to pass*

Namath, Joe

Before the Super Bowl in 1969, Joe shocked fans by predicting that his Jets would beat the Baltimore Colts. He shocked them more when he and the Jets actually did it.

Playing with an injured knee, Namath (number 12) throws his first touchdown pass for Alabama in the 1965 Orange Bowl. Although he set an Orange Bowl record of 18 pass completions, Alabama lost to Texas, 21–17.

the game, Joe Namath was being honored as American Football League (AFL) Player of the Year. Joe's ready tongue already had him in hot water for putting down the National Football League (NFL) quarterbacks. Joe had accused them of building up their pass-completion percentages by throwing short little passes to their backs. He had said that there were four AFL quarterbacks—including himself—who were better than the Colts' NFL Player of the Year, Earl Morrall. At the banquet he turned to his league's president and asked, "How can you guys say it's wrong to have long hair?" Then he turned to the audience and talked about the upcoming game.

"The Jets will win on Sunday! I guarantee it," he said flatly. That kind of talk ends up on opponents' locker room walls. But Joe had an answer for that. If the Colts needed incentive to win a Super Bowl, he added, then they were in real trouble.

In the Super Bowl, Namath was superb. He had one of the great arms in football, but he saved his strategy for the ground wars. He avoided the blitzing Colts, who had hoped to knock him silly early in the game. He kept sending Jets fullback Matt Snell at the Colts' right defensive end. The Jets

and Colts sparred for the rest of the quarter. There was no score yet, but the Jets gained a mental advantage. In the two previous Super Bowls, the AFL teams had been scored on early, and then had never caught up. In the second quarter, Namath guided Snell in for a touchdown (TD). The Jets led, 7–0, at the half.

The Jets picked up a field goal in the third quarter. Then Namath passed into the end zone for a TD that was called back. After the throw, he was slammed into by a Baltimore lineman and had to leave the game. But Namath had left the team in field-goal range. The Jets moved ahead 13–0. Namath came back on the field and, wisely eating up time on the ground, guided the Jets in for a third field goal. They now led 16–0. The Colts fought back and got a touchdown. But

Namath, Joe

meanwhile, Namath kept using up time by running the ball or throwing short passes. The final figures showed him with 205 yards through the air, but nobody will remember that. What will be recalled is the Jets' stunning 16–7 victory. Joe was named the game's Most Valuable Player (MVP).

As Joe looked up to the Orange Bowl stands, he saw many of the 75,000 fans screaming madly for him and his Jets. "The people cheering," he said, "are the same people who were betting against us, who said we didn't have a chance."

That was the real Joe Namath—frank, outspoken, and cocky, but a man who could back up his words.

Career Highlights

Totaled more than 40 collegiate touchdowns at the University of Alabama

Named 1965 American Football League (AFL) Rookie of the Year in 1965

Set a single-season passing record by tossing for 4007 yards in 1967

Led the New York Jets to the 1969 Super Bowl, pulling off a dramatic upset over the heavily favored Baltimore Colts

Elected the 1969 Super Bowl MVP and AFL Player of the Year

Inducted into the Football Hall of Fame in 1985

Ups and Downs

In a career marked by injury and controversy, Namath did not rank very high among the statistics that measure great quarterbacks. Following the 1977 season—his last in professional football—Namath had completed just over 50 percent of his passes. Others, like Bart Starr, Len Dawson, and Fran Tarkenton, had hit their receivers about 57 percent of the time. Joe had been intercepted more than 200 times in 13 seasons, a poor mark. He had thrown for 173 touchdowns and 27,663 yards. But less than one out of every 20 of his passes had gone for a TD. Still, many fans felt Namath was the best quarterback in the game.

After his great performance in Super Bowl III, Namath had made believers out of his skeptics. He received the Hickok Belt as the year's top professional athlete. At the end of the 1969 season, the AFL and the NFL merged. The Pro Football Hall of Fame conducted a poll to pick an "All-Time All-AFL team." Joe Namath, who had played in only half of the AFL's 10-year existence, was named as quarterback.

Early Life

Joseph William Namath was born in the steel mill town of Beaver Falls, Pennsylvania, on May 31, 1943. He had three older brothers who became football players. Beaver Falls is in the heart of a high school football hotbed. Between the brothers and the locale, there

In his five years in the old American Football League, Namath passed for a total of 15,487 yards.

Getting set to use his quick release, Namath passes against the New York Giants in a preseason game.

was no trouble getting young Joe interested in the game.

Joe's first sport was baseball. He began in junior leagues at 6 and spent his spare time tossing footballs to his older brothers. Joe Namath was 5-feet tall and weighed 115 pounds when he tried out for the football team in junior high. He could hardly see over the linemen's outstretched arms to find his receivers. Because he was so small, there were not many positions he could play. In high school, he became discouraged because he did not play much. His parents kept insisting that he attend practice regularly so that the coaches would know he was there.

As a junior he became a starter and a star. As a senior he became a superstar, leading Beaver Falls High School to an unbeaten season. He completed over 60 percent of his passes, and the college recruiters were after him. Joe was outstanding in basketball and baseball, too. He could have signed a good bonus contract with the Chicago Cubs. But his father, who grew up working in the steel mills, did not want to see his son end up there if he failed in baseball.

Joe Namath chose the University of Alabama. His career with the Crimson Tide was a blend of problems, injuries, and brilliant football. He threw 29 TD passes as a three-year starter, and he scored 15 more on the ground. The highlight of his career came in his final game, when he sparked the Crimson Tide in the 1965 Orange Bowl against the University of Texas. Joe completed 18 of 37 passes for 255 yards and two TDs in a strong, but losing, effort. He was the star of the game.

Already the pros had their eyes on him. The New York Jets desperately needed a drawing card for their new AFL franchise. The St. Louis Cardinals of the NFL needed a quarterback. A bidding war broke out, much to Joe's delight.

Making the Pros

Joe Namath ended up with a Jets contract worth about $400,000. That was a lot of money to pay for a pro athlete at the time, equal to

Namath, Joe

A famous football player, Namath also has played in Hollywood movies. Here he rides a motorcycle in C.C. and Company.

about $2.2 million in 2002. But the Jets began to get their investment back in a hurry as season ticket sales soared. Namath started slowly with the Jets, then came on to win Rookie of the Year honors.

"What we like about him is that he's a winner," said Jets coach Weeb Ewbank. "He doesn't know about losing."

Leading the Way

Before long, Joe took complete charge of the Jets on the field. He accepted blame when it was due and gave credit to his teammates when the club won. There was enough credit for him, too. New York named him "Broadway Joe," and women chased after him. Advertising people sought him to endorse their products. Joe's plush apartment, flashy cars, long hair and beard, and his zestful bachelorhood were the talk of New York. "If you got it, flaunt it," he said in a television commercial, and that was the way he lived.

Injuries on the field came thick and fast. Sportswriters spent as much time interviewing the doctors as they did the coaches when they wanted to find out about Joe. Many times his career seemed to be at an end. But somehow he would always come through with another stunning effort. During the 1972 season, he completed 15 passes for 496 yards and six touchdowns in a game against the Baltimore Colts. That year, the Colts had one of the best zone defenses in football.

But in his last years at New York, Namath did not have the support that helped him win in the 1960s. Although he passed for an impressive amount of yards in 1974 and 1975, his completion rate was low. Slowed down by his bad knees, Joe became a better target for defensive linemen each year.

The hard knocks eventually took their toll on Namath. He was waived by the Jets in 1977. He then signed with the Los Angeles Rams. Broadway Joe spent one year with the team and retired in January 1978.

When asked about Namath, legendary coach Paul "Bear" Bryant replyed: "He is the greatest athlete I have ever coached."

"You learn you can do your best even when it's hard, even when you're tired, and maybe hurting a little bit. It feels good to show some courage."

—Joe Namath

In 1969, Joe Namath was asked by football commissioner Pete Rozelle to give up his share in a New York restaurant. Rather than give up the restaurant, Namath decided to retire from football. Here, he makes his tearful announcement in front of three of the most famous sportscasters in the business: Frank Gifford (left), Kyle Rote (second from right), and Howard Cosell. Namath did not stay retired long.

Not only one of the biggest sports heroes in New York, Namath also hosted a popular sports program on television. Here he chats with another famous sports star, Muhammad Ali (center).

Further Study

BOOKS

Chadwick, Bruce. *Joe Namath.* New York, NY: Chelsea House Publishers, 1995.

Sanford, William R. and Carl R. Green. *Joe Namath.* New York, NY: Crestwood House, 1993.

WEB SITES

"Joe Namath," *Pro Football Hall of Fame.* Online at www.profootballhof.com/index.cfm?section=team&cont_id=player&personnel_id=1309&roster_id=42 (November 2003)

Navratilova, Martina

Martina Navratilova (1956–   ), tennis player, was born in Prague, Czechoslovakia. Martina's stepfather taught her to play tennis when she was a young child. She began competing outside of her own country as a member of the Czech Tennis Federation. Martina defected to America during the 1975 U.S. Open. She defeated Chris Evert to win the women's singles title at Wimbledon in 1978. Her titles included the Australian Open (1981, 1983, 1985), the French Open (1982, 1984), Wimbledon (1978, 1979, 1982, 1987, 1990), and the U.S. Open (1983, 1984, 1986, 1987). Martina won six straight Grand Slam tournaments—three each in 1983 and 1984. Navratilova teamed with Pam Shriver to form the greatest doubles pair in tennis history. In 2003, Martina won her 20th title at Wimbledon, winning the mixed doubles with partner, Leander Paes of India. When she defected in 1975, the 19-year-old Czechoslovakian sought freedom and opportunity. But unlike most immigrants, she had an advantage in her new country. She was already on her way to fame and fortune as one of the greatest tennis players in the world.

Martina Navratilova was born October 18, 1956, in Prague, Czechoslovakia. (In 1993 her native country broke apart into two countries, the Czech Republic and Slovakia.) By the time she was 2 years old, her parents had her on skis. By the time she was 6, a tennis racquet was almost always in her hand. Martina's idol was Billie Jean King.

As a youngster, Martina had high hopes of becoming a tennis star. "When I was six or seven, I started dreaming about being number one," she recalled. "I always had faith in my talents. When I was eight or nine, and not really

Navratilova concentrates as she returns a shot during a doubles match in 2001.

Sanex

Navratilova, Martina

With Billie Jean King (right), Martina won the Wimbledon women's doubles title in 1979.

good for my age, my [step]father said I would win Wimbledon some day."

Her stepfather, Mirek Navratii, was her first coach. He taught her to play the game aggressively. Instead of playing from the baseline, Martina would charge the net with abandon. It took her several years to master the style.

"Everybody said I was crazy," Martina later explained. "I was losing and losing, but I was still attacking. Then as I grew, I began cutting off passing shots with my volleys. My serve got stronger. I began to win."

Political Problems

As her game improved, the political situation in Czechoslovakia deteriorated. One day in 1968, tanks stormed into the town of Pilsen, where Martina was visiting a friend. Russian soldiers had been ordered into the country to crush a Czech revolt. Nervous soldiers were ready to shoot at anything that moved. Martina went into hiding. That night, Mirek rescued Martina on his motorcycle and whisked her back to their hometown of Revnice.

In 1973, Martina made her first trip to America as a 16-year-old member of the Czech Tennis Federation. As she began to travel more and more, she became a political suspect in her own homeland. Tennis officials and secret police scrutinized her moves. She had to give a large portion of her tennis earnings to the federation. Worse yet, tennis officials told her where she could and could not play. She wanted the freedom to decide herself.

At the 1975 U.S. Open at Forest Hills, New York, Martina officially renounced her Czech citizenship and asked for political asylum. By then, Navratilova had become an international tennis star. She had made the finals of the French, Australian, Italian, and German opens.

Navratilova serves during the 1975 U.S. Open. She asked for political asylum in the U.S. during the tournament.

Navratilova had her first banner year in 1975. She posted an 88–21 record in singles play and was ranked as the fourth-best player in the world. She also earned $184,668 (equal to about $650,000 in 2002) in prize money. Navratilova became

Navratilova displays the women's singles trophy at Wimbledon in 1978. She defeated Chris Evert, 2–6, 6–4, 7–5 to take the title.

known as the strongest of the women players.

A Difficult Period

A year later, Martina became depressed. Although she had settled into her own home in Dallas, Texas, she missed her family and native land. Her weight rose from 145 to 170 pounds. Martina's mental and physical state affected her performance on the court. Her earnings were cut almost in half. She did, however, share the 1976 Wimbledon doubles crown with Chris Evert.

Martina relaxed and felt more at home in 1977. She benefited from the friendship and counsel of former pro golfer Sandra Haynie, who became her business manager. Martina also got back to the business of winning tennis matches, earning more than $300,000 for the year. (Adjusting for inflation, $300,000 would equal about $900,000 in 2002.)

The one thing Navratilova wanted most, however, was the singles title at Wimbledon. After making it to the quarter finals in 1977, Martina decided to bear down in practice sessions and competition. She also decided to lose some weight. A year later, she made it to the Wimbledon finals and faced her friend Evert.

Making a Dream Come True

Martina lost the first set, 2–6. Early in the second set, she ran directly into a cross-court volley. "It hit me on the temple," she said. "It didn't hurt, but it woke me up."

Navratilova won the second set 6–4. She started strong in the third set, but Evert caught her and took the lead, 4–2. Then Martina went on the attack and emerged a 7–5 victor. She had, at last, become the Wimbledon champion. After her victory, she stated, "My win was a win for Czechoslovakia."

At the end of 1978 season Navratilova had the best record in women's tennis. She had

"A lot of people have been number one for a while, but not too many people have stayed there. I'm going to be one of those people who is able to stay up there."
—Martina Navratilova, who held the number one ranking for 156 consecutive weeks

Navratilova, Martina

broken Evert's all-time marks by winning 37 consecutive matches and 7 straight tournaments on the Virginia Slims circuit, a series of major tennis tournaments. She won 11 of the 18 tournaments she entered in 1978. She also earned $443,540, which put her over the million-dollar mark in career winnings.

Navratilova was rated the top woman tennis player in the world in 1978. It marked the first time in five years that Evert did not achieve the ranking.

"A lot of people have been number one for a while," Martina remarked. "But not too many people have stayed there. I'm going to be one of those people who is able to stay up there."

Career Highlights

Holds record of nine Wimbledon singles championships

Won six straight Grand Slam titles from 1983 to 1984

Won 18 total Grand Slam singles titles

Owns 161 career singles titles, the most in history

Along with Pam Shriver, had a 109-match winning streak in doubles during the 1980s

Tied with Billie Jean King for most career Wimbledon titles (20)

Elected to International Tennis Hall of Fame in 2000

Struggling to Stay on Top

She was true to her word. In 1979, Martina captured the finals of the Avon Championships in New York City. At Wimbledon that year, she won her second consecutive singles title and teamed with Billie Jean King to take the women's doubles title. Navratilova earned $747,548 in 1979, topping the list of money-winners for the second year in a row.

One of Martina's greatest thrills did not occur while playing tennis. It did, however, take place at Wimbledon in 1979. There, she was happily reunited with her mother, Jana, whom she had not seen since defecting in 1975.

Navratilova dropped to third in the rankings in 1980 and 1981. Although she possessed the most talent on the women's circuit, she suffered mental lapses that kept her from playing her best. In 1981, she fell apart at the Toyota Championships and at the U.S. Open after establishing huge leads. Martina lacked concentration at times and, thus, consistency. Tennis authority Ted Tinling told *World Tennis Magazine*, "Navratilova goes from arrogance to panic with nothing in between."

A New Era

The year 1981 was a turning point in Martina's life and career. She not only was granted U.S. citizenship, but also gained thousands of fans and admirers. Her following became apparent at the U.S. Open, where she lost an extremely close final to Tracy Austin. Following the match, Navratilova received a tremendous ovation from the crowd that left her in tears.

Meanwhile, basketball player Nancy Lieberman had become Navratilova's trainer. Nancy believed Martina was wasting her talent, in large part because of poor training and practice habits. So, Nancy put her on an intense conditioning program. Soon, Martina was in the best shape of her life She was 145 pounds of sheer muscle.

Navratilova recalled, "Nancy just wouldn't let me sit still. I'd say, 'I can't go on anymore.' I'd start crying, literally, because I was so

Martina Navratilova won her eighth Wimbledon singles title in 1987. Later that year, at the U.S. Open, she won her 50th Grand Slam title. That total included 17 singles championships.

tired. She knew where my limit was better than I did."

In addition, former tennis player Renee Richards became her coach. She overhauled Martina's game, shot by shot. (Richards was replaced in 1983 by Mike Estep, another former pro.) "Team Navratilova," as her entourage came to be known, also included a nutritionist.

Martina's hard work helped her build a steel-edged confidence in her game. She won 15 of 18 tournaments in 1982. Overall, her record was 98–3. Navratilova captured her third Wimbledon crown in 1982, defeating Chris Evert Lloyd, 6–1, 3–6, 6–2. She also won her first French Open title and, with Pam Shriver, became part of one of the most potent doubles combinations in women's tennis.

Navratilova was even better in 1983. She won three legs of the Grand Slam and earned a record $1,456,030—more than three times as much prize money as her nearest competitor. She posted a phenomenal record of 86–1.

Martina's victories were astonishing in their ease. At Wimbledon, Navratilova raced through seven matches in five and a half hours without losing a set. She crushed Andrea Jaeger in the final, 6–0, 6–3, in just 54 minutes.

Next was the U.S. Open, the only major tournament that had eluded her. The Open had become an obsession with Martina. She had said, "I don't think winning the Grand Slam is necessary, but the U.S. Open is. That's the one thorn in my side."

Martina was at her best at the 1983 Open. She displayed a flawless serve-and-volley game and an array of masterful shots, from powerful serves to keenly accurate passing shots. She demolished Chris Evert Lloyd in the final, 6–1, 6–3.

Ahead of the Game

The gap kept widening between Navratilova and the rest of the players on the women's circuit. Beginning in 1983 and ending in 1984, she had a 54-match winning streak—the second-longest in history. The great Billie Jean King said, "Martina is head and shoulders above everybody."

Navratilova won the 1984 Virginia Slims Championship, defeating Evert Lloyd, 6–3, 7–5, 6–1. The event was the first best-of-five match for women in over 80 years. Later, Martina beat Chris for the first time ever on clay, 6–2, 6–0.

At the 1984 French Open, Martina had a chance to become only the fifth tennis player in history to win the Grand Slam (Wimbledon and the U.S., Australian, and French opens). The previous winners had captured the Grand Slam in the same calendar year. In 1982, however, the International Tennis Federation (ITF) changed the official interpretation of the Grand Slam. The ITF stated that it would recognize anyone who won the four major tournaments consecutively.

Navratilova gained the Grand Slam, tennis's ultimate achievement, by defeating Evert Lloyd in the French Open final, 6–3, 6–1. Her 63-minute victory followed her singles titles at Wimbledon, the U.S. Open, and the Australian Open. (She also won the tournaments in doubles, with Pam Shriver.)

In the match, Martina lost her serve only once and wore down Evert Lloyd with a succession of deadly drop shots. "I tried to look for weaknesses and I couldn't find any," said Chris after the match.

Martina continued to confirm her place as perhaps the greatest player in the Open era. In 1984, her loss at the Australian Open ended her bid for a record seven straight Grand Slam titles and ended her consecutive match winning streak at a record 74. In 1987, she won her sixth straight Wimbledon title and her fourth U.S. Open. Martina captured a record ninth Wimbledon singles crown in 1990. She credited her new coaches, Craig Kardon and Billie Jean King, for helping her. Meanwhile, Martina and Pam Shriver had become the best doubles team in women's tennis history. The duo won a record 20 Grand Slam doubles titles.

Navratilova has remained involved in tennis, still playing doubles on the WTA circuit. She shattered more records in 2003, winning the mixed doubles competition at Wimbledon, becoming the oldest (at age 46) to win a Wimbledon title. The victory also gave her 20 Wimbledon career titles, tying her with Billie Jean King for the career record. Off the court she has remained busy as well. Beginning in 1995, Martina has been seen as a commentator for HBO coverage of Wimbledon. She also has written five books about her tennis career and her involvement in both women's and gay rights. "Navratilova's impact has been huge," said Shriver. "She helped women realize they can work and push themselves physically to a much higher level." Monica Seles added, "Martina's been a leader, on and off the court."

Further Study

BOOKS

Herzog, Brad. *The 20 Greatest Athletes of the 20th Century.* New York, NY: Rosen Publishing Group, 2003.

Zwerman, Gilda. *Martina Navratilova.* New York, NY: Chelsea House Publishers, 1995.

WEB SITES

"Hall of Fame Enshrinees," *International Hall of Fame.* Online at tennisfame.com/enshrinees_atoz.html (November 2003)

The strongest player on the women's tennis circuit, Martina unleashes her awesome serve.

The Record Book

Tennis (women)

Wimbledon titles, career

1. Martina Navratilova	***20***
Billie Jean King	20
2. Elizabeth Ryan	19
3. Suzanne Lenglen	15
4. Louise Brough	13

Wimbledon singles titles, career

1. Martina Navratilova	***9***
2. Helen Wills Moody	8
3. Steffi Graf	7
Dorothea Lambert Chambers	7
5. Blanch Bingley Hillyard	6
Suzanne Lenglen	6
Billie Jean King	6

Most singles tournament titles, career

1. Martina Navratilova	***14***
2. Chris Evert	12
3. Steffi Graf	11
4. Margaret Court	11
5. Billie-Jean King	10
6. Evonne Goolagong	65
7. Virginia Wade	55
8. Monica Seles	53
9. Martina Hingis	40
10. Lindsay Davenport	38

Most Grand Slam singles titles, career

1. Margaret Court	24
2. Steffi Graf	22
3. Helen Wills Moody	19
4. Martina Navratilova	***18***
Chris Evert	18

Records current as of February 2004

Nelson, Byron

Byron Nelson (1912–), golfer, was born in Fort Worth, Texas. He won the Southwest Amateur golf tournament when he was 18. Two years later, he turned professional. Nelson started his rise to the top with a victory in the 1937 Masters tournament. He posted victories in the U.S. Open in 1939 and the Professional Golfers' Association (PGA) title in 1940. Nelson won his second Masters in 1942 and added another PGA title in 1945. Nelson's most memorable accomplishments occurred during 1945 and 1946. Over a period of 18 months he won 18 tournaments, including 11 in a row. During his brief but remarkable career, he won 52 PGA tournaments, which ranks fifth on the all-time list.

Before the days of Tiger Woods, if you had to choose the best golfer of all time, you could make a strong case for Byron Nelson. During his brief pro golf career, he continually set records—many of which may never be broken.

His career total of tournament wins was 54—ranking fifth for all time. This is especially remarkable since he retired at the age of 34, a few weeks after a caddie's error cost him the 1946 U.S. Open. Nelson's caddie accidentally kicked his ball, causing him to suffer a penalty.

His retirement came at the peak of his game. He was second only to Ben Hogan in money earnings. In the 1940s, Byron Nelson finished in the money 113 straight PGA tournaments—a record that was broken by Tiger Woods in 2003.

In 1945 and 1946, Nelson won 18 tournaments, averaging 68.23 strokes per round. Eleven of those tournament wins were consecutive. He captured one right after another. Also during that year, he stroked the fantastic score of 66 in 19 different rounds.

In 18 blazing months, Byron Nelson never shot worse than par for 72 holes. Famed golfer Bobby Jones remarked after seeing Nelson play, "At my best, I never came close to the golf Nelson shows."

Nelson's straight-victory record is unlikely to be equaled. Today there are more tournaments, but there are also many more fine golfers competing to win.

"Actually, I won 19 tournaments, 12 in a row in 1945," Nelson said, "but later it was discovered that an event in Spring Lake, New Jersey, did not meet minimum purse requirements. The total purse was $2,500. The Professional Golfers' Association (PGA) then had a minimum of $3000."

Byron Nelson was born on February 4, 1912, the son of a grain merchant. He grew up in a home near the Glen Garden Club in Fort Worth, Texas. When Byron was a youngster, he began caddying at the club golf course.

Nelson tees off in the first round of the 1945 Victory National Open.

He quickly learned the game, and at 14, he tied for the caddie championship with another 14-year-old—Ben Hogan.

Two years later, young Byron won the Glen Garden Club's junior title. At 18, Byron Nelson hinted at his future potential by capturing the Southwest Amateur crown.

Turning Pro

He turned pro in 1932, and in his first tournament, the Texarkana Open, he tied for third. Nelson was only 20. But five lean years followed. Then, in 1937, Nelson won his first Masters tournament. He was well on his way to an incredible, if short, career.

At the Masters, Nelson showed his great putting skills. He sank a 30-footer on the 10th hole, beginning a charge to overtake Ralph Guldahl's four-stroke lead. Within two holes, Byron Nelson picked up six strokes on Guldahl.

In the 1939 Open, Nelson tied Craig Wood after 72 holes of play. They were still deadlocked after the first 18-hole playoff. Then, on the 453-yard fourth hole during the second playoff, Nelson hammered his tee shot 240 yards down the middle. His next shot was a low drive—again down the middle. The ball rolled onto the green and stopped against the pin that held the flag. Nelson carefully pulled out the pin. The ball plopped in for an eagle-2. Wood, shaken by the shot, played badly the rest of

"At my best, I never came close to the golf Nelson shows."

—Golf legend Bobby Jones

Nelson, Byron

The Record Book

Golf

Most tournament victories, season

1. Byron Nelson	***18***	***1945***
2. Ben Hogan	13	1946
3. Sam Snead	11	1950
4. Ben Hogan	10	1948
5. Arnold Palmer	8	1960
Johnny Miller	8	1974

Most tournament victories, career

1. Sam Snead	81
2. Jack Nicklaus	70
3. Ben Hogan	63
4. Arnold Palmer	60
5. Byron Nelson	***52***

Records current as of February 2004

the round. Byron Nelson won the Open.

In the 1940 PGA, Nelson beat his old caddying rival, Ben Hogan, in the quarter finals. In the finals, he finished one stroke ahead of Sam Snead to win.

In 1942, he joined Horton Smith and Jimmy Demaret as the only repeaters in the Masters. Nelson did it the hard way—by beating Ben Hogan in one of the greatest playoff matches ever staged.

After the halfway point, Hogan successfully chewed away Nelson's eight-stroke lead. Nelson and Hogan met for a playoff. In the first five holes, Ben Hogan moved ahead by three strokes. But beginning with the sixth hole, Nelson turned on some incredible golf and gained five shots on Hogan in 11 holes—even though Hogan had completed those 11 one under par. The round finished with Nelson at 69 and Hogan at 70. Nelson took home his second green jacket for winning the Masters.

Nelson suffered from hemophilia, a condition that keeps the blood from clotting. In 1940, the United States started a military draft, and all men had to register for it upon their 18th birthday. When Nelson registered for the military draft, he was given a 4-F draft classification, which meant he could not be drafted because of his hemophilia. So, unlike most of his friends, he did not serve in World War II (1939–45). The 1943 tour was canceled because of the war, so Nelson spent the year teaching golf at Cleveland's Inverness Club.

The tour was resumed in 1944. Although many of the pros were in the service, par was still par, and Nelson continued to wreck it. He averaged 69 strokes and won $40,000 from the small war-time purses. The Associated Press named him Athlete of the Year.

The next year was his most impressive. Because of his consistent below-par play, he was being called "The Mechanical Man" and "Lord Byron."

No one has ever played better golf than Byron Nelson did from early in 1945 to late summer in 1946. He was suffering from back trouble but still managed a record-breaking tour.

In the 1945 PGA, Nelson routed Gene Sarazen, Denny

Career Highlights

Captured two Masters titles (1937, 1942)

Won two PGA Championships (1940, 1945)

Won eleven tournaments in a row from 1945–46

Won 54 career tournaments, fifth on the all-time list

Elected to the Professional Golf Hall of Fame in 1974

Has a PGA tournament, the Byron Nelson Classic, named in his honor

Byron Nelson watches confidently as he knocks in this putt to win the 1946 Victory National Open.

Shute, Claude Hannon, and Mike Turnesa. He had trailed Turnesa by two strokes with only four holes to play. Nelson then charged home with a par, two birdies, and an eagle to win. For the fifth time in six years, he reached the PGA finals.

During the final match, he easily defeated Sam Byrd. Byrd later said, "Byron is the best ever."

It was his last PGA tournament win. But he had set a still unbeaten PGA record-shooting a 68.33 strokes-per-round average for 120 rounds in a row.

Retirement

Byron Nelson's back trouble was getting severe. It was agony for him to crawl out of bed each morning. He began missing tournaments. When he arrived in Portland, Oregon, for the 1946 PGA, he had to lean on his wife for support.

He retired soon afterward. But he took with him crowns from one U.S. Open, two PGAs, and two Masters, as well as numerous small tournaments.

"I decided in February after winning the San Francisco Open that I would quit. I had won every title I could in the United States. Golf had nothing left for me. But I played on for six more months. For all my victories, I was unable to save anything. I had to get into more profitable work."

After retiring, he rejoined the tour only for the Masters in Augusta, Georgia, and made an occasional appearance at the Bing Crosby tournament at Pebble Beach, California. Byron was second in the 1947 Masters, and he won the Crosby in 1951.

Even as he grew older, he retained his golf touch. In 1973, on a par-3 course, the 61-year-old shot two rounds. Playing in the rain, he finished the 18 holes in 46.

A major PGA tournament is named in his honor, the Byron Nelson Classic.

Further Study

Davis, Martin. *Byron Nelson*. New York, NY: Broadway Books, 1997.

Nicklaus, Jack

Jack Nicklaus (1940–), golfer, was born in Columbus, Ohio. He received his first golf clubs at 10 and started taking lessons from a local pro. In high school, he excelled in basketball and baseball as well as golf. While attending Ohio State University, Nicklaus won National Amateur titles in 1959 and 1961. In 1962, his first year on the professional tour, he won the U.S. Open. From the early 1960s and into the 1970s, he dominated the world of golf. He won three more U.S. Open titles (1967, 1972, 1980), five Professional Golfers' Association (PGA) Championships (1963, 1971, 1973, 1975, 1980), six Masters titles (1963, 1965, 1966, 1972, 1975, 1986), and three British Open tournaments (1966, 1970, 1978) in three decades. Five times he was named PGA Player of the Year. His 20 major championship victories is a record and he is the only golfer to win all four major titles at least twice. Nicklaus has kept on winning tournaments since joining the Senior PGA Tour in 1990. Considered by many as the greatest golfer in history, Jack Nicklaus also designed golf courses, some of which are ranked among the finest in the world.

Most experts agree that Jack Nicklaus is the greatest golfer of all time. His remarkable record speaks for itself.

The first golfer to pass the $5-million mark in career earnings, Jack was eight times the leading money-winner on the tour. Five times he was named the Professional Golfers' Association (PGA) Player of the Year (1967, 1972, 1973, 1975, and 1976). He won six Masters titles, five PGA Championships, four U.S. Open titles, three British Opens, and a pair of National Amateur titles. He is the only man to capture all four major championships twice.

His greatest effort may have been his record sixth Masters triumph in 1986. He roared past

Finishing high, Nicklaus follows the flight of the ball.

Nicklaus, Jack

eight players, surging from four strokes back after three rounds, to win by one stroke. He shot a 65 in the last round and a record-tying 30 on the back nine. That 30 included five birdies and an eagle. Nicklaus called his comeback "as fine a round of golf as I've ever played."

Jubilant upon winning the 1965 Masters, Nicklaus turns and throws his ball down the 18th fairway.

Early Life

Jack William Nicklaus was born January 21, 1940, in Columbus, Ohio, the son of an owner of a chain of drugstores. His father encouraged him to compete in sports and prodded him by betting he could not win. "Once dad told me I was too fat to win a race in junior high," Nicklaus recalls. "So I entered and won three races."

When he was 10, his father gave him a set of clubs, and he set out at once for the Scioto Country Club. There, Jack shot a 51 for nine holes. He then started taking lessons from Jack Grout, the head pro. At 16, Jack Nicklaus won the Ohio Open.

In high school, Jack was outstanding in baseball and basketball. He connected on 90 percent of his free throws and averaged 18 points a game as a guard on the basketball team. Yet he always favored golf.

"I have seen many big fellows in my time, but they all had some weakness. Jack doesn't have any."
—golf great Bobby Jones

During the World Series of Golf in 1970, Nicklaus blasts out of a trap on his way to first place.

"Playing other sports helped my coordination," explained Nicklaus. "I have strong arms and legs, and I've worked hard to get them into my swing. I never have stopped practicing.

"I played an exhibition with Sam Snead at the Urbana (Ohio) Country Club when I was 16," he said. "I shot a 72; Sam had a 68. We were about the same off the tee, but Snead's irons were so accurate. I couldn't help but absorb some of his rhythm. It would have been more fun if Sam hadn't kept calling me 'Junior.'"

Jack received scholarship offers from a dozen colleges. But on his father's advice, Jack decided to attend Ohio State University without benefit of any aid. A business administration major, Nicklaus worked at his father's stores during vacations.

Winning Recognition

National recognition came to Jack in 1959. Early in the year, he was named to the nine-man American amateur team for the Walker Cup matches against a British team. "The goal of every amateur is to make the Walker Cup team," said Nicklaus. "Simply being selected for it gave me a new confidence in myself." Jack won both his matches as the American team defeated the British at Muirfield, Scotland.

With his new found confidence, Nicklaus lost only once in 30 matches that year. In September, he won the National Amateur title at Colorado Springs by defeating defending champion Charlie Coe at the 36th hole.

The next year, Nicklaus led the Americans to a World Amateur Team championship. He posted a blazing 11-under-par 269 at the Merion Golf Course in Pennsylvania. He also finished second to Arnold Palmer in the 1960 U.S. Open. In 1961, Jack won a second National Amateur title. After his victory, Jack entered the professional ranks.

His first tour victory came in June of 1962. In the U.S. Open at the Oakmont course in Pennsylvania, Jack battled favorite Arnold Palmer to a 283 tie at the end of 72 holes. In the playoff round that followed, Palmer fans jeered and taunted the crew-cut rookie from Ohio, much to the embarrassment of Arnold. Jack won the round,

Nicklaus, Jack

71–74, becoming the youngest Open champion since Bobby Jones's 1923 victory. A World Series of Golf win later that year proved the burly youngster was one of the best on the tour.

In 1963, Jack became the youngest player to win the Masters, finishing with a 2-under-par 286. But his game was still a bit erratic. He failed to qualify for the U.S. Open but won the PGA Championship at Dallas, Texas.

Nicklaus placed second in the Masters, the PGA, and the British Open in 1964. Although without a "major" victory, Jack finished the year as the leading money-winner.

The next two years, Jack won the Masters. It was the first time anyone had taken the title in successive years. His score in 1965 was a record 271—17 strokes under par—it stood until 1997 when Tiger Woods shot a 270. That course seemed tailored to the powerful Nicklaus game. Whenever Jack played there, people expected him to win. Another of Jack's favorite courses is Muirfield in Scotland, the site of his first British Open victory in 1966.

At the Baltusrol Golf Course in New Jersey, Nicklaus took the 1967 U.S. Open. His 275 was the lowest total ever posted in the event's 67-year history. Jack was named PGA Player of the Year in 1967.

Keeping Perspective

The Ohioan did not win another major tournament until 1970. "We all go through certain periods of being down," he said later. "I was down for nearly three years. Golf didn't seem to be much fun anymore."

During those years, Nicklaus rearranged his business affairs and gradually changed his appearance and image. In the early days, Jack lived with such nicknames as "Whaleman" and "Ohio Fats." He was called the "Golden Bear" not only for his blond hair and ferocious play, but also for his bulky build. By 1970, he had lost much of that weight. His hair was longer and his clothes more fashionable. In his spare time, he played tennis and basketball to keep in shape. And once again, he began to play golf with the skill and concentration that everyone knew he had.

Back On Top

Nicklaus came out of his slump with a win in the 1970 British Open at St. Andrews, Scotland. Jack finished the 72 holes tied with Doug Sanders at 283. In the playoff round, he bested Sanders

Jack holds the trophy presented to him as champion of the 1972 U.S. Open.

The Record Book

Golf

Most major titles, career

1. Jack Nicklaus	***18***
2. Walter Hagen	11
3. Gary Player	9
Ben Hogan	9
5. Tom Watson	8
Tiger Woods *	8

Most tournament victories, career

1. Sam Snead	81
2. Jack Nicklaus	***70***
3. Ben Hogan	63
4. Arnold Palmer	60
5. Byron Nelson	52

** Still active*
Records current as of February 2004

With power and determination, Nicklaus drives off the ninth tee during first-round action of the 1971 U.S. Professional Match Play Championship.

by a single stroke. The following year, Nicklaus won the PGA Championship, while finishing second in both the Masters and the U.S. Open.

In 1972, Nicklaus won the Masters by three strokes and battled bad weather to take the U.S. Open at Pebble Beach, California. There was talk of a sweep of the major tournaments—the Masters, the U.S. Open, the British Open, and the PGA—golf's "Grand Slam." But Jack's hopes were dashed as Lee Trevino beat Nicklaus in a tough battle at the British Open. He finished the year with the most tournament victories and was named PGA Player of the Year.

Through the next two years, he won only one major title, the 1973 PGA Championship. But he was again selected PGA Player of the Year in 1973. By then, Jack Nicklaus was acknowledged by everyone as the best golfer in the world. Always known for his power off the tee, he had developed into one of the best putters in the game. His concentration was unmatched. Golfers who played with him at times were exasperated by his careful study of each shot. It was Jack who began the practice of obtaining the precise yardage of each approach shot. He would then file away the information for future reference.

Nicklaus almost won the Grand Slam in 1975. He took the Masters and the PGA. He finished one stroke back in the British Open and ended two strokes behind the winner in the U.S. Open. The leading money-winner on the tour, Jack was again named Player of the Year. "I'm probably a better player now than I ever was," said Nicklaus.

In 1976, he again won the Player-of-the-Year award, although he did not win a major tournament. Jack did take the Tournament Players Championship and the

Nicklaus, Jack

World Series of Golf. He became the leading money-winner for the eighth time.

From Golfer to Golf Course Designer

One of his main interests was golf course architecture. His affection for Muirfield in Scotland was evident when he built a course outside his hometown of Columbus. Jack named the new club Muirfield Village. As head of Golden Bear International, Nicklaus eventually designed over 100 top-rated golf courses all over the world.

At Muirfield Village in May 1977, Jack captured his 63rd PGA tournament victory, placing him second on the all-time list. Calling the Memorial Tournament at Muirfield his greatest victory, Nicklaus went over the $3-million mark in career earnings. No other golfer in history had made even $2 million on the professional tour.

In 1978, Jack Nicklaus won his third British Open championship and was named Sportsman of the Year by *Sports Illustrated.* He suffered his worst season on the PGA tour in 1979. But Jack was back in 1980. He captured his fourth U.S. Open title, shooting a record 272 for the tournament. He also won his fifth PGA Championship.

Aside from tournament play, Nicklaus also represented the United States in the international

Nicklaus sends the sand flying at the 1986 Masters tournament. The 46-year-old golfer won the event, marking his 20th major title.

Career Highlights

Won National Amateur Championships in 1959 and 1961

Five-time PGA Champion

Emerged victorious in six Masters championships (1963, 1965, 1966, 1972, 1975, 1986)

All-time leader in major tournament wins with 20

Has hit 18 holes-in-one during career

Nicklaus demonstrates the form that has made him one of the longest drivers in golf history.

competition for the World Cup. Four times with Arnold Palmer (1963, 1964, 1966, 1967), once with Lee Trevino (1971), and once with Johnny Miller (1973), Jack helped win the Cup for the United States.

When Jack Nicklaus won his 20th major at the 1986 Masters, he had not captured a PGA tournament since 1984. After his victory, the 46-year-old champion said, "This [Augusta] is a young man's golf course. But it is also a course where experience helps you. I was able to use my experience today." He added, "I just want to be occasionally as good as I once was. Today, I was."

The great Jack Nicklaus had 71 career victories on the PGA tour—second only to Sam Snead. But more important, Jack's 20 major championship wins were an all-time record and seven more than second-place Bobby Jones.

The great Nicklaus remained active after his prime, joining the Senior PGA Tour and winning 10 of the first 35 tournaments he entered. The Golden Bear has also made several instructional video tapes called "Golf My Way." Jack Nicklaus has been actively involved in Nicklaus Design, a company that has designed and created hundreds of elite golf courses. Without question, Jack Nicklaus's involvement in the sport of golf is unmatched and he will forever be remembered as a true legend.

Further Study

BOOKS

Shaw, Mark. *Nicklaus.* Dallas, TX: Taylor Publishing Company, 1997.

Wukovits, John. *Jack Nicklaus.* Philadelphia, PA: Chelsea House Publishers, 1998.

WEB SITES

"Jack Nicklaus," *CNNSI.com: GolfPlus.* Online at sportsillustrated.cnn.com/golf/pga/bios/2003/bio154.html (November 2003)

Nishiyama, Hidetaka

Hidetaka Nishiyama (1928–), karate master, was born in Tokyo, Japan. He earned a black belt in judo at 14. He began his formal training in karate at 17, studying under Master Gichin Funakoshi, who introduced the discipline to mainland Japan from the island of Okinawa in 1922. Nishiyama attended Takushoku University in Tokyo and captained the school's karate team from 1947 to 1949. Later, he helped found the Japan Karate Association and became a karate combat instructor for the Strategic Air Command of the U.S. Air Force. He moved to the United States in 1961 and became associated with the All-America Karate Federation. Settling in Los Angeles, California, Nishiyama established a dojo (school) for serious karate students. In the 1970s, he served in executive positions with the Pan American Karate Union and the International Amateur Karate Federation. Dedicated to karate as a mental as well as a physical discipline, Hidetaka Nishiyama has taken his teaching to countries all over the world. In *kumite,* a type of karate competition, Nishiyama has never been defeated.

Karate is often misunderstood by people whose only exposure to it has been a few hours of motion picture and television viewing. Karate has been abused, especially in the United States. It has become equated with violence and ferocity, and a means for attack. The *do* aspect—the polite, truthful, gentle, and fearless way of life that karate teaches—is seldom stressed. Dishonest instructors and phonies pretend to teach karate rapidly. Many commercial *dojos* (schools) do not even teach the traditional forms called *kata.* Often, a student learns only a few techniques and quickly begins fighting.

Hidetaka Nishiyama hoped to protect karate from that attitude and approach. He worked for many years to convey the true meaning of karate. Nishiyama dedicated himself to an ideal far beyond sport, competition, or even martial art. He dedicated

In karate sparring competition, Hidetaka Nishiyama has never been defeated.

"A man who has ascended to his pinnacle, that is to the limit of his capability, but who still remains unproficient, is a better man than the person who has the potential, but has stopped short of his summit to bask in some of the glories of his achievement."

—Hidetaka Nishiyama

Nishiyama, Hidetaka

himself to an ideal of self-realization that embraces the best of man's world.

History of Karate

Karate, a descendant from Chinese combat techniques, is several hundred years old. It is a martial art of self-defense that uses the human body in the most effective way. Blocking, punching, striking, and kicking techniques are used in combination with other related movements. More than a sport, karate is a self-discipline in which victory itself is not the ultimate goal.

The introduction and growth of karate came after World War II. It was due to public awareness of its value in physical education and self-defense. The first karate competition was held in 1956 in Japan. Since then interest has rapidly grown.

Supporting the Sport

Hidetaka Nishiyama has been in the center of the karate boom. In the United States, he has been an active instructor and karate organizer since 1961. Students travel thousands of miles to train in his central dojo in Los Angeles, California. The students are dedicated to the highest level of karate achievement: physical and mental self-discipline aimed at the perfection of character. A few that Nishiyama judges adequately prepared are sent to foreign countries to carry on the work of teaching the highest quality karate.

Nishiyama has also been the executive director of the International Amateur Karate Federation (IAKF), executive director of the Pan American Karate Union, and chairman of the All America Karate Federation (AAKF).

Early Life

Hidetaka Nishiyama was born on November 21, 1928, in Tokyo, Japan. He attained his black belt in judo at 14, and began studying karate at 17. Karate was then still relatively unknown even in Japan. He began his formal training under Master Gichin Funakoshi, who introduced modem karate to Japan from Okinawa, in the Ryukyu Islands, in 1922.

In 1945, Nishiyama became a member of the strong collegiate team at Takushoku University in Tokyo. From 1947 to 1949, he served as team captain. While studying at the university for six years, Nishiyama's schedule included morning, afternoon, and evening karate training daily. In 1950, he founded, organized, and became the first chairman of the Japanese Collegiate Karate Union. In 1951, he graduated from the university with a master's degree in commercial science and became one of the founders of the Japan Karate Association.

Career Development

At the invitation of the United States Air Force, Nishiyama served as a combat instructor in karate for members of the Strategic Air Command (SAC). In 1953, he toured the SAC bases in the United States giving demonstrations and checking the quality of instruction. His demonstrations of karate coincided with the karate boom in the United States during the 1950s.

Career Highlights

Earned a black belt in judo at only age 14

Founded the Japan Karate Association

Combat instructor for the United States Air Force

Organized the first All America Karate Federation Championship Tournament

Has never been defeated in Kumite competition

Returning to Japan, Nishiyama became chief of the instruction department for the Japan Karate Association. He wrote his first book on karate in 1959 with Richard C. Brown. He has also written other books highly prized by karate enthusiasts all over the world.

In November 1961, Nishiyama settled in the United States. He soon organized the first All America Karate Federation (AAKF) Championship Tournament, held in the Los Angeles Olympic Auditorium. Later, he planned and hosted the first AAKF United States versus Japan Championship. Held in San Francisco, California, it was the first international karate competition in the United States. Later, he sponsored the first International Invitational Karate Championships in Mexico City, the first international competition on a world scale. This competition created the foundation for the organization of international karate. It also helped standardize quality karate—one of Master Nishiyama's long-term goals.

For years Nishiyama has worked to get karate accepted as an Olympic sport.

Through his efforts at organizing, administrating, mediating, as well as instructing, the AAKF became a member of the U.S. Olympic Committee in 1972. The following year, the Pan American Karate Union was formed with Nishiyama as executive director.

Goals and Achievements

Other achievements in world karate followed. In 1974, he became executive director of the nonprofit International Amateur Karate Federation (IAKF). The organization's World Karate-do Championships, held at Los Angeles in 1975, marked the first time that a tournament operated under internationally established rules and regulations. The Pan American Karate Union, under his direction, was recognized as the sole karate-controlling body for the Pan American Games.

Nishiyama is constantly flying around the world attending to his responsibilities. He travels often on weekends so he will miss teaching as few classes as possible. His classes include morning, afternoon, and evening sessions. He has taken his teaching and organizing skills to countries all over the world.

Hidetaka Nishiyama is planning for the future. There is work to be done in the IAKF, which includes over 60 countries. He also works to strengthen the various karate regions. His major goal is the inclusion of karate in the Olympic Games.

Nishiyama is working for the international expansion of his karate organization. But he is quick to make it clear that his work is always guided by the underlying spirit of the traditional martial art, a standard of excellence without compromise. The approximately 30,000 members of the AAKF look toward the realization of that goal.

Further Study

BOOKS

Nishiyama, Hidetaka and Richard C. Brown. *Karate: The Art of "Empty Hand" Fighting.* Rutland, VT: C.E. Tuttle Company, 1974.

WEB SITES

"Master Hidetaka Nishiyama," *International Traditional Karate Federation.* Online at www.itkf.org/tkbody.aspx?catid=1101(November 2003)

Nurmi, Paavo

Paavo Nurmi (1897–1973), distance runner, was born in Abo, Finland. At 15, his idol was the great Finnish distance runner Hannes Kolehmainen. By the 1920 Olympic Games in Antwerp, Belgium, Nurmi was also a great distance runner. He won gold medals in the 10,000 meters and the 10,000-meter cross-country race and a silver medal in the 5000 meters. He set two Olympic records in less than an hour when he ran the 1500- and 5000-meter races at the 1924 Games in Paris, France. He won four individual gold medals in the 1924 world competition. In 1925, Nurmi made his famous trip to the United States where he established 38 indoor records in 55 meets and earned his nickname, "The Flying Finn."

In the 1928 Olympic Games in Amsterdam, The Netherlands, Nurmi won nine gold medals and three silver medals in Olympic competition. He set 35 world records in 16 different events in a career spanning a little more than a decade. When he retired, Paavo Nurmi had set world records for everything from 1500 to 20,000 meters.

Fact and fiction are hard to separate in the career of Paavo Nurmi, probably the greatest runner who ever lived. A host of stories and legends abound about this outstanding Finnish athlete. In their telling, truth has sometimes been displaced by rumor, or even sheer invention.

One rumor said Nurmi divorced his wife because she refused to allow the feet of their son to be stretched so that the little boy might become a faster runner. Another tale charged Nurmi with accepting $25,000 (equivalent to almost $250,000 in 2002) for a series of indoor races in the United States. Still another claimed Nurmi ate nothing but black bread and fish. Another rumor charged Nurmi had slowed down to permit a fellow Finn to win a race.

Only the accusation of taking money bothered The Flying Finn, because such talk might endanger his amateur status. In fact, late in his career, a charge that he had accepted excess expense money caused his downfall in 1932. The world track organization—the International Amateur Athletic Federation (IAAF)—barred him from the Olympics. Until that time, Nurmi had ruled the track for more than a decade.

But one part of the Nurmi legend was true past all question. That was his record as a runner on the track.

Nurmi won nine Olympic gold medals and three silvers in the Olympic Games of 1920, 1924, and 1928. Seven of those gold medals were in individual events and two in relays. He set world records in 16 different events and in one relay. All told, he broke world records 35 times.

Paavo Nurmi set two world records in the short period of two hours. In a meet in Helsinki in 1924, Nurmi won the 1500 meters in 3:52.6, then came back to win the 5000 meters in 14:28.4.

In one tour of U.S. indoor tracks, The Flying Finn set 38 indoor records in 55 meets. During this tour, he was accused of taking home a bagful of money as well as a bagful of medals. His fast speed in distance events was often attributed to his low heart rate (40 beats per minute compared to the average man's 72). The unkind joke went around, "Nurmi has the lowest heart beat and the highest asking price."

Early Life

Paavo Nurmi was born on June 13, 1897, in Abo, Finland. When he was 15, his idol was the great Finnish runner Hannes Kolehmainen, who had won four Olympic distance races.

Nurmi's father died when Paavo was 12, and the youth grew up in poverty. He became a vegetarian for lack of meat, not by choice. Nurmi had to help his family earn money by doing errands and odd jobs. At the end of the day, he was crammed into a one-room cottage with five other people. It was a hard life for a young boy, but it also toughened Paavo for the task of becoming a great distance runner.

As a soldier in 1918, he is said to have run 15 kilometers (over 9 miles) in full military gear with a knapsack full of sand in less than one hour. He ran every day, and by 1920 he was ready to take on the world.

That year at Antwerp, Belgium, Nurmi finished second in the Olympic 5000 meters to French runner Joseph Guillemot. Three days later, the two met again in the 10,000-meter race. Nurmi trailed going into the home stretch, but then he kicked out with a burst of speed and won by eight yards. He proved himself again in the 10,000-meter cross-country race, winning by four yards. In Finland, where distance runners are idolized, Paavo returned home a hero.

He continued to train hard at his running. He carried a stopwatch in practice and later in races so that he developed an exact sense of pace. He would run his own race as he had planned it in advance. Often, in the home-stretch, he would toss his watch to the side of the track and break into a sprint to the finish line.

Olympic Games, 1924

At the 1924 Olympics in Paris, France, Nurmi was the number-

"Mind is everything. All that I am, I am because of my mind."
—Paavo Nurmi

Nurmi, Paavo

one attraction. He did not disappoint the fans.

He was the world record holder in the mile run with a time of 4 minutes, 10.4 seconds (4:10.4)—a record that was to stand for eight years. Naturally, he was a heavy favorite to win the 1500-meter event, a distance about 100 yards short of a mile. He had only one problem. The 5000-meter race, in which he also was the world's best, was the same afternoon as the 1500-meter race—with less than an hour between them.

Nurmi so far outclassed the field in the 1500 that he slowed down to an easy lope in the final lap. At one point, he was 40 yards ahead of his nearest rival. Had he not slowed, he would have surely smashed his world record in the 1500. Instead, he settled for a clocking of 3:53.6, about one second away from the record.

As the crowd cheered and the other runners huffed and puffed after the race, Nurmi looked fresh but poker-faced. He darted straight to the locker room, after picking up his sweatsuit and the stopwatch he had discarded when the outcome of the race was certain.

He rested, got a massage, and—as one reporter from Chicago wrote—"munched on bits of dried fish." Then, to a roar of welcome, he returned to the track 50 minutes later to take part in the 5000 final.

One of his competitors there was a fellow countryman, Willie Ritola, considered second only to Nurmi among world runners. Paavo and Willie had little love for each other. Legend tells that on the first day of the 1924 Olympics, Nurmi, who was not allowed to run the 10,000-meter race, trotted over that distance in a practice run while Ritola was winning the official gold medal race. Legend also claims that Nurmi recorded a much faster time than Ritola's world record—30 minutes, 23.2 seconds.

Nurmi was ready for the 5000-meter final. He watched Ritola and a Swede named Edvin Wide pull out in front at the start of the race. Nurmi trailed by as much as 30 to 40 yards. But "Peerless Paavo" knew what he was doing as he constantly checked his stopwatch. He did not intend to let the others burn him out. About halfway through the race, Paavo took the lead for the first time.

Ritola, equally determined, ran in Paavo's shadow. Nurmi stepped up his speed to a furious pace. Ritola stayed with him. With 20 yards to go they were even. Then Paavo dipped into his reserve of energy and broke for a final spurt. He won by a yard. The track world had never seen a better effort in one hour's time.

Nurmi was the victor in another race—the 10,000-meter cross-country run. Then he took on Ritola again in the 3000-meter team race and carried home the victory.

Keeping In Motion

The next year, 1925, Nurmi made his historic tour to the United States. He would compete in New York one night, hop a train to compete in Chicago the next, then

Career Highlights

Won 9 gold medals (6 individual) in 1920, 1924 and 1928 Olympics

From 1921–31 broke 23 world outdoor records in events ranging from 1500 to 20,000 meters

Established 38 indoor records after arriving in the United States

Has a marathon and track-and-field meet named in his honor in his native Finland

Nurmi carried the torch into the stadium at the start of the 1952 Olympics in Helsinki, Finland.

shoot back to New York by train for his third appearance in three evenings.

It was not an easy schedule to keep, but Nurmi stuck to his training as much as he could. At one outing, given by Finnish-American citizens, Nurmi was asked to join in a toast.

"I never drink liquor or use tobacco," he said.

"But this is for the honor of Finland," said the toastmaster.

"Where will the honor of Finland be if I lose my next race?" snorted Paavo, and added bluntly, "Pass the coffee."

Nurmi continued to win. He captured the 10,000 meters at the 1928 Olympics, beating Ritola's record, but he lost the 5000. It was said that he allowed a teammate to beat him in the steeplechase.

Controversy Arises

Then Paavo Nurmi was suspended from taking part in the 1932 Olympics—as the result of an inquiry into his expense accounts three years earlier. Nurmi's heart had been set on winning a marathon. The steely-eyed runner broke down and wept when he failed to get reinstated.

"If I did something wrong, why did they wait three years before taking action?" he asked. "Why turn on me now, when my heart bleeds to end my career by winning the marathon?"

Not until two decades had passed did Nurmi receive official forgiveness. At the 1952 Olympics in Helsinki, Finland, Nurmi was given the honor of bearing the Olympic torch into the stadium.

Today a statue of the great Flying Finn stands near the entrance to the Helsinki stadium. It serves to remind his countrymen and others that a tiny, northern land of rocks, lakes, and birch trees produced "the greatest long-distance runner of all time."

Peerless Paavo Nurmi died quietly in Helsinki, in the land of his birth, on October 2, 1973.

Further Study

BOOKS

Uschan, Michael V. *Male Olympic Champions*. San Diego, CA: Lucent Books, 2000.

Oakley, Annie

Oakley, Annie (1860–1926), markswoman, was born Phoebe Anne Oakley Mozee in Greenville, Ohio. She learned to shoot at the age of 8 with her father's 40-inch cap-and-ball Kentucky rifle. In 1875, she defeated the noted marksman and vaudeville performer Frank E. Butler in a shooting match in Cincinnati.

Several years later, Phoebe married Butler and joined his shooting act under the name of Annie Oakley. 1880, the Butlers joined Buffalo Bill's Wild West Show. Annie broke her first 100 straight traps in an 1887 match race in London, setting a club record. Annie went on to set records in trapshooting for 20 years.

The 1970s was a decade of "women's liberation." By 2000, women were doing things that were once done only by men. This is especially true in sports. But over 100 years ago, one sportswoman established herself as a top competitor for a period of almost 50 years. Annie Oakley was one of the best, male or female, ever to shoot a gun, and her feats have become a legend.

Annie Oakley was so good with a gun that she once performed her magic in front of seven crowned heads of Europe in one day. Among her most treasured trophies was a cup of solid silver awarded by Edward VII, England's Prince of Wales at the time. On it he had enscribed "You are the best shot I have ever seen."

An idea of her value, even as a woman in the late 1800s, may be better understood when it is realized that she asked for and got $700 a week during her tour of Europe. She also won $9000 in two years of trapshooting, during a time when money was hard to come by and her appearances at tournaments were limited.

Annie Oakley's worth with a gun was recognized right from the beginning. Born Phoebe Anne Oakley Mozee (Moses) on August 13, 1860, in Greenville, Darke County, Ohio, she was the sixth of eight children. Her father, Jake Mozee, was a Pennsylvania farmer who had moved to Ohio. When Annie was only 4, her father died. For the next few years the family suffered in poverty. Her mother married a mail carrier, but money was still very hard to earn. So, at age 9, Annie took to the woods with her father's old 40-inch cap-and-ball Kentucky rifle and began shooting quail and rabbits. Even then she proved to be a deadly shot.

Her kill was shipped off to Cincinnati, Ohio, and the money Annie received was used to help the family. In just five years, her earnings paid off the mortgage on the Mozee family farm.

By the time Annie was 15, in 1875, she was locally famous as the best markswoman in the area. Her friends arranged for her to go to Cincinnati to compete in a contest with Frank E. Butler. Butler was a noted marksman and vaudeville performer. He thought the whole thing was a joke, but soon learned otherwise. The little girl from the backwoods defeated the famous rifleman by one point. Although defeated on the shooting range, Butler soon fell in love with Annie, and they were married several years later.

In private life she was Mrs. Frank Butler, but she joined her husband's shooting act and became known as Annie Oakley.

Annie and Frank Butler joined the Four-Paw and Sells Brothers Circus in 1880 and performed their shooting act together. They traveled all over the country. In 1882, they arrived in St. Paul, Minnesota. There they met the great Sioux Indian chief, Sitting Bull. He and his people were so impressed with Annie Oakley's marksmanship that they adopted her into their tribe. They called her "Mochin Chilla Wytonys Cecilia," the Sioux name for "My Daughter, Little Sure Shot."

In 1884, Annie Oakley and Frank Butler joined the Wild West Show. They traveled with this group run by "Buffalo" Bill Cody for 17 years.

The Wild West Show made a tour of Europe in 1887, and Annie set a club record in London by shooting 100 straight at trap in a match race.

The Wild West Show was overseas for 17 months and Annie is given credit for saving it. She gave two performances a day, seven days a week. When the show began to run out of money and seemed headed for failure, Annie put up $8000 of her own money to save it.

Annie Oakley once performed before seven crowned heads of Europe, winning numerous medals for her shooting.

A master with a gun, Annie could hit the target by shooting backwards, using only a mirror with which to see.

Flawless Accuracy

Annie Oakley was a master with a gun. At 30 paces she could slice a playing card with the thin edge toward her. If someone threw a dime in the air she could shatter it with a single shot. One of her most dangerous acts was a favorite with the crowds. Her husband would hold a cigarette in his mouth between his lips and Annie would shoot it out. She could fill a playing card that had been thrown in the air with a dozen holes. In fact, the term "Annie Oakley" is still used to describe complimentary tickets of all kinds because of the punch holes.

One of Annie's favorite tricks was to lie on her back and have her husband throw six glass spheres in the air at once. Using three loaded double-barrel shotguns, she would shatter all six before they hit the ground.

She was severely injured in a train wreck in 1901 and was partially paralyzed. Yet in the 25 more years she was to live, she added to her great shooting records. In 1921, she had a car accident and had to wear a brace the rest of her life. However, a year later she still broke 100 clay targets.

Annie died in Greenville, Ohio, on November 3, 1926. She was cremated and her ashes placed in a trophy she had earlier won at the Universal Exposition in Paris. Just 20 days after her death, her husband Frank also passed away.

The long career of Annie Oakley spanned a time when many changes were being made in America. She made her mark with her gun and has been remembered in movies and a TV show. Her skill with a rifle and shotgun may never be matched.

Oh, Sadaharu

Sadaharu Oh (1940–   ), baseball player, was born Wang Cheng-chih in Tokyo, Japan. As a high school pitcher, he led his team every year to the national tournament. He joined the Yomiuri Giants of Japan's Central League in 1959 as a first baseman. After three mediocre seasons with the Giants, Oh developed his unorthodox batting style of lifting his front leg up as he stepped into a pitch. During his career, Oh led the league in home runs 15 times and in runs batted in (RBIs) 13 times. He also won five batting crowns and two Triple Crowns. On nine occasions, he was named the league's Most Valuable Player (MVP). Sadaharu Oh surpassed Henry Aaron's all-time home run mark of 755 in 1977. Oh retired following the 1980 season with 868 lifetime home runs.

If a baseball player were to lead his league in home runs for more than a dozen straight seasons, every fan in America would know him and make him a hero. If this same player were to break the all-time home run record of 755 set by Henry Aaron, he would be acclaimed on the front page of every newspaper in the country.

Such a player was not make-believe. He did exist. But many American baseball fans never heard of him. His name was Sadaharu Oh and he played first base. However, one never saw him play on the Game of the Week, nor did one read much about him in the local newspaper. The reason is that Sadaharu Oh played for the Yomiuri Giants in Japan's Central League. Playing games in Japan's capital city of Tokyo, Sadaharu Oh was the most famous sports star in the nation. In Japan, baseball is as popular as it is in the United States. Oh's picture and endorsement were on all kinds of products.

Oh joined the Yomiuri Giants in 1959 and was used sparingly in 94 games. The fans were given little to notice about Oh as he hit for a very poor .161 average. But he made only four errors in the field the entire season. In 1960, he boosted his average to .270 and knocked in 71 runs.

Still, neither the fans nor the Yomiuri Giants had much to get excited about when the name Sadaharu Oh was mentioned. But Oh knew he had the talent to be an outstanding baseball player.

Born less than two years before his countrymen attacked Pearl Harbor and declared war on the United States, Oh spent the first years of his life in a nation totally involved in war. The exact date was May 20, 1940, when Sadaharu Oh was born in Azuma-cho, Sumidaku, Tokyo, of a Chinese father

Oh leaps for joy after breaking Babe Ruth's record by hitting his 715th home run in 1976.

and Japanese mother. His original name was Wang Cheng-chih.

Even in war-ridden countries, little boys can find happiness. Sadaharu Oh loved baseball, a game that was quickly becoming popular in Japan, and he was strong enough to play it all the time. He entered Waseda Business High School and joined the baseball squad as a pitcher. Leading his team to the National High School Tournament every year, Oh pitched a no-hitter and hit home runs in two consecutive games. Because Oh was doing so well in a relatively new sport, he was becoming nationally famous.

Developing His Skills

From 1959 through 1961, Sadaharu Oh was just another player on the Yomiuri Giants. But suddenly in 1962, the tough little first baseman developed a new batting technique. Oh was a left-handed batter. Suddenly, with every pitch, he would lift his right leg high in the air just as the ball reached the plate, much like former New York Giant star Mel Ott. This enabled him to throw all his weight into his swing, and the amazing results were immediate.

In just one year, Sadaharu Oh raised his home run total from 13 to 38 and upped his runs batted in (RBIs) total from 53 to 85. Both totals were tops in Japan's Central League. By 1963, he was hitting .305, and he would not drop below .300 for the next seven years.

"He sure hit me. He was a superb hitter. He hit consistently, and he hit with power."

—Hall of Fame pitcher Tom Seaver, after facing Oh in an exhibition game

Oh, Sadaharu

(below) With the increased popularity of baseball in Japan, bubble gum cards are also in great demand. One of the favorite collector's items is, naturally, Sadaharu Oh.

(left) This was the famous Sadaharu Oh batting style —lifting his right foot just as the ball reached the plate.

Career Highlights

Led Japan League in home runs 15 times

Won the Japan League Triple Crown twice

Elected a nine-time MVP while playing for the Yomiuri Giants

Hit 868 home runs in 22 years, most in baseball history

Has more RBIs than any player in Japanese history

During the 1967 exhibition season, the Yomiuri Giants played the Atlanta Braves in Vero Beach, Florida. Here, Sadaharu Oh watches the flight of the ball as he heads for first base.

A Steady Success

From then until the end of his career, Oh's yearly home run total did not drop below 30. His highest output came in 1964, when he belted 55 homers. For 14 seasons, he knocked in 100 or more runs. He drove in a career high 124 in 1977. Oh also led the Giants to 12 Japan Series crowns, including an unprecedented nine straight titles from 1965 through 1973.

"He's 36 years old and right now he'd hit 35 to 40 homers if he were in the majors," said former Cleveland Indians pitcher Bob Feller, who witnessed Oh's 716th home run in 1976. "Kids skip school just to look at him, to be near him. You can't pick up a newspaper or magazine without seeing his picture....They even televise his batting practice."

The great Sadaharu Oh broke Henry Aaron's major league record of 755 home runs in 1977. When Oh retired after the 1980 season, he had a lifetime batting average of .301. He had also collected 278 hits and 2170 RBIs. Nine times the Central League's Most Valuable Player, Oh slugged 868 homer during his 22-year career.

Further Study

BOOKS

Oh, Sadaharu. *A Zen Way of Baseball.* Norwalk, CT: Easton Press, 1998.

Ohno, Apolo Anton

Apolo Anton Ohno (1982–), short-track speed skater, was born June 22, 1982, in Seattle, Washington. The young speed skater thrilled audiences across the world during the 2002 Winter Olympics in Salt Lake City, Utah. Ohno won two medals during the Games; gold in the 1,500 meters and silver in the 1,000 meters. His unique name, youthfulness, and good looks made Apolo Anton Ohno an Olympic hero and crowd favorite. Prior to the 2002 Winter Olympics, Ohno was a three-time United States champion and 1,500-meter world record holder. In 2001 he was the World Cup overall champion—the youngest American (age 17) to win a World Cup event. After the Olympics he continued to excel, capturing back-to-back U.S. titles in 2002 and 2003.

The sport of short-track speed skating made its Olympic debut in 1994 at the Lillehammer games. A fast, intense sport, skaters zip around a small track. As a result, crashes and collisions are common. Skaters reach speeds of up to 30 miles per hour using custom skates with long, sharp blades. Apolo Anton Ohno describes his sport like this: "It gets pretty crazy, pretty wild. It's fast with a lot of passing. And then a skater will lose an edge or get bumped and go down. It's real exciting, very dynamic."

Born and raised in Seattle, Washington, Apolo Anton Ohno is the son of Yuki Ohno and Jerrie Lee. He received his name from his Japanese father, who combined the Greek words "apo" and "lo" to create Apolo. The name translates into the phase "to lead away from." Anton roughly means "priceless." Apolo Anton Ohno's mother, Jerrie Lee, is of American descent. Apolo's parents divorced when when Apolo was a 1 year old. Yuki Ohno took sole responsibility for his son.

As a teen, Apolo was rebellious and often in trouble. However, he was also involved in athletics and excelled in swimming. At age 12, he was a state champion breaststroke swimmer. Ohno also excelled in in-line skating. However, in 1994, a new sport caught his attention.

Apolo and his father were watching the Winter Olympics in Lillehammer, Norway on television. They found one event particularly interesting: short-track speed skating. The sport was new to the Olympic games and not well known in the United States. Yuki

Apolo Anton Ohno leads Fabio Carta of Italy around the track during competition in the men's 5000-meter relay at the 2002 Winter Olympics.

"He skates with such confidence that even his competitors can't help but envy him and admire him at the same time."

—Cathy Turner, former speed-skating gold medalist

Ohno, Apolo Anton

Ohno turned to his son and said, "Why don't you give short-track a try?" Apolo liked the idea and set out to become a speed skater.

He was a natural. By age 13, Apolo was one of the top skaters in the world. Despite his success, he continued to surround himself with negative influences, including older friends who were gang members. In an attempt to protect his son—and jumpstart his speed-skating career—Yuki Ohno made plans to send Apolo to the U.S. Olympic training camp in Lake Placid, New York. Apolo, however, did not want to go. Yuki took Apolo to the airport expecting him to board a plane for Lake Placid. Apolo had other ideas. After his father left, he called a friend to pick him up and take him home. Yuki, however, finally convinced Apolo that Lake Placid was where he should be.

Apolo hated training in Lake Placid. He was forced to run, lift weights, and spend long hours on the track. He also felt strange living in a town much smaller than his native Seattle. But Ohno adjusted. Eventually he got used to the strenuous schedule, and began to enjoy training and preparing for the 1997 U.S. Championships.

Career Highlights

Five-time U.S. Speed-Skating Champion

U.S. record holder in the 500 meter race

Two-time Olympic medalist

World Cup Overall Champion in 2001 and 2003

Youngest American to ever win a World Cup event

Into the Spotlight

Apolo Anton Ohno won his first major competition at the 1997 U.S. Championships. The victory made Ohno set his sights on competing in the 1998 Winter Olympics in Nagano, Japan. However, he failed to train properly and was not included on the U.S. Olympic Team. The disappointed Ohno was devastated. But he had only himself to blame.

He went alone to a quiet cabin in the woods near Seattle. While there he pondered his future. He decided to take the sport seriously and dedicate himself to winning.

His new attitude paid off. Ohno made the team for the 1998 World Championships. A year later, he recaptured the U.S. Championship and, in 1999, he won the World Cup. At age 17 he was the youngest American ever to win the event. He secured his position in the sport by winning back-to-back U.S. Championships in 2000 and 2001.

Apolo Anton Ohno leads his heat to win the quarterfinals of the men's 500-meter qualifying round at the 2003 World Cup. Ohno was the overall champion of the event.

Olympic Star

Ohno entered the 2002 Winter Olympics as a favorite to win medals for the United States in short-track speed skating. Olympic fans, some of whom had never heard of the young skater, became enamored with the 5-foot, 8-inch, 165-pound teenager. His good looks were accented by a distinctive soul patch (a small patch of hair under his lower lip). The soul patch became Ohno's trademark. Hundreds of fans in the stands wore paper imitations on their faces.

In his first race, the 1,500 meters, Ohno went up against Kim Dong Sung of South Korea, one of the best skaters in the world. The closely contested race came down to the final meters.

Kim Dong Sung crossed the finish line first. It appeared that Ohno would be awarded the silver medal. Controversy followed, however, as the judges disqualified the Korean for blocking Ohno from passing. Ohno, as a result, was awarded the gold.

The 1,000-meter race was equally intense. Coming around the final turn of the track, the skaters, including Ohno, became tangled. There was a massive crash in the home stretch and Apolo fell to the ice. During the collision, a sharp skate blade sliced his leg and cut it open. Determined to win, Apolo crawled across the finish line, winning the silver medal. In an emotional moment, Ohno was pushed to the medal ceremony in a wheelchair after receiving stitches in his injured thigh.

Post Olympic Popularity

Americans fell in love with Ohno during the Olympics. The governor of Washington even declared May 14, 2002, Apolo Anton Ohno Day.

Despite his success and popularity, Ohno remains a normal guy. He enjoys spending time with his father, who he views as his strongest influence. He likes hanging out with friends, listening to music, and breakdancing. When he isn't training, Apolo takes high school courses from an on-line academy.

With youth on his side, Ohno has a bright future. He is expected to dominate the U.S. speed-skating scene and star in the next Olympic Games. Cathy Turner, former speed-skating gold medallist, said of Apolo Anton Ohno: "He skates with such confidence that even his competitors can't help but envy him and admire him at the same time. He is the intimidator. He is the one to beat. He is the extraordinary one to watch."

Further Study

BOOKS

Lang, Thomas. *Going For the Gold—Apolo Anton Ohno: Skating on the Edge.* New York, NY: Avon Books, 2002.

Layden, Joe. *All About Apolo!* New York, NY: Aladdin Paperbacks, 2002.

Ohno, Apolo Anton and Nancy Richardson. *A Journey: The Autobiography of Apolo Anton Ohno.* New York, NY: Simon and Schuster Books for Young Readers, 2002.

Olajuwon, Hakeem

Hakeem Olajuwon (1963–), basketball player, was born in Lagos, Nigeria, in Africa. He played soccer as a youth and was perhaps the world's only 7-foot goalie. He played basketball for only a few months before coming to the United States in 1980. Tutored by Moses Malone, Olajuwon helped lead the University of Houston basketball team to the NCAA Final Four three times. Olajuwon left college after his junior year and joined the Houston Rockets. He was the first pick in the 1984 NBA draft. In his early pro seasons, Olajuwon averaged over 20 points a game and ranked among the league's top 10 in rebounds, steals, and blocked shots. He led the Rockets to the 1986 NBA finals, averaging almost 25 points in the championship series. Possessing size, strength, quickness, and speed, Hakeem Olajuwon led the league in rebounding in 1989 and 1990. It was in 1994 and 1995 that the Rockets finally got enough firepower to support Olajuwon, winning the NBA championship both years. He retired in 2002.

One day in 1980, 7-foot, 190-pound Akeem (later known as Hakeem) Olajuwon arrived at the airport in Houston, Texas. The young African had come for an interview with the University of Houston coach, but no one bothered to meet the 17-year-old at the airport. After all, he was not such a hot prospect—he had played basketball for only a few months.

In Houston, Olajuwon improved his crude skills at the Fonde Recreation Center. There, in the summers, he and National Basketball Association (NBA) star Moses Malone began working out together.

Malone took the skinny novice under his wing and taught him some painful lessons on the court. Moses would elbow and shove Akeem, all the while chiding, "You gotta want the ball. Fight me. Fight me."

Within a year, Olajuwon was playing his mentor to a virtual standoff. It was only the beginning

Hakeem "The Dream" possessed a rare combination of power and grace that led to many easy dunks such as this.

Carl's
FOX SPORT
34
ROCKETS

"Olajuwon is the main Rocket launching pad, erected down low, where he is spinning, jump-hooking, and power-dunking his way to greatness."

—Jack McCallum

Olajuwon, Hakeem

of Akeem's meteoric rise in the basketball world.

Early Years

Akeem Olajuwon was born January 23, 1963, in Lagos, Nigeria, on the west coast of Africa. He was one of six children. His parents, Abik and Salaam, ran a successful cement business. Akeem grew up playing soccer and became a fine goalie. By the time he finished his studies at Moslem Teachers College (the equivalent of high school) in Lagos, he spoke French, some English, and four Nigerian dialects.

When Akeem joined the Cougars, his natural ability was obvious. But he was a raw talent with limited knowledge of the game. But Akeem improved rapidly. He got tough. He also got heavier, increasing his weight to 240 pounds with a diet that featured steak, ice cream, and jellybeans.

Career Development

In three collegiate seasons, Olajuwon helped lead the Cougars to three Final Four appearances and two National Collegiate Athletic Association (NCAA) championship games. In Houston's final two games of the 1983 NCAA tournament, Akeem totaled 41 points and 40 rebounds. He was voted the tournament's Most Valuable Player (MVP). As a junior, he led the nation in blocked shots with an average of 5.6 per game.

Akeem Olajuwon turned professional following his junior year, joining the Houston Rockets. He was the first player chosen in the 1984 NBA draft. Olajuwon guided Houston to a 48–34 record as a rookie. The team had posted a 29–53 mark the previous year.

Olajuwon possessed everything a team could want in a big man: quickness, strength, soft hands, leaping ability, and the speed and stamina to run the floor. He also had supreme confidence to make the big play, the mark of the truly great ones. And above all, he had "the desire to be on top," which was the literal English translation of his family name, Olajuwon.

Akeem "The Dream" was a joy to watch. On offense, he moved with grace, whether executing the drop-step he had learned from Malone and slamming the ball through the basket, or dipping a shoulder, whirling one way then back the other, and shooting a fade-away jumper. He was smooth.

Olajuwon was a terror on defense. He specialized in stealing the ball or ripping down a rebound, making an outlet pass, and racing down to the offensive end of the court to take a return pass for a power dunk.

"In terms of raw athletic ability, Akeem is the best I've ever seen," gushed Magic Johnson. "I'm amazed at his fakes, his pivot moves, his timing on blocked shots, his scoring ability, and his effort."

Career Highlights

All-America selection in 1984 and Final Four Most Outstanding Player in 1983 for the University of Houston

Overall first pick by Houston Rockets in 1984 NBA draft

Led the Rockets to back-to-back NBA titles (1994 and 1995)

Named regular season MVP (1994) and two-time Finals MVP (1994 and 1995)

Six-time All-NBA first team (1987–89, 1993–95)

All-time NBA blocked shots leader (3830)

Olajuwan became one of the NBA's most graceful centers.

A Rocket is Launched

In his first two pro seasons, Olajuwon averaged over 21 points and more than 11 rebounds per game. He ranked among the NBA leaders both years in rebounds and blocked shots. In the 1986 playoffs, he led Houston past the Los Angeles Lakers in the Western Conference finals, scoring 40 points and 35 points in two of the contests.

The next season, Olajuwon was named to the All-NBA first team at center—his first of three straight selections. He was also named to the league's All-Defensive first team for the first time.

In 1987–88, Olajuwon was the only player to finish in the top ten in four categories—scoring, rebounds, blocks, and steals. That year, he set a playoff record for points (150) in a four-game series.

Within a month in 1990, he scored a career high of 52 points in one game and achieved a rare quadruple-double when he totaled 18 points, 16 rebounds, 11 blocks, and 10 assists in another contest.

In 1991, Olajuwon changed his first name to Hakeem. "It's no big deal," he said. "I just wanted to go back to using the original spelling." In Arabic, Hakeem means "a wise man; a doctor."

"Hakeem Olajuwon is a mixture of brute and ballet dancer," wrote Jack McCallum in *Sports Illustrated.* "He is the main Rocket launching pad, erected down low, where he is spinning, jump-hooking, and power-dunking his way to greatness."

Olajuwon did all those things en route to greatness. He played 18 seasons, the last with the Toronto Raptors, before retiring following the 2001–02 season. "The Dream" poured in 26,946 career points, good for seventh all-time. He stands atop the all-time blocks list, swatting away 3,830 shots in a magical career.

Further Study

BOOKS

Christopher, Matt. *On the Court With Hakeem Olajuwon.* Boston, MA: Little, Brown, 1997.

Knapp, Ron. *Sports Great Hakeem Olajuwon.* Springfield, NJ: Enslow Publishers, 2000.

WEB SITES

"Hakeem Olajuwon," *NBA History.* Online at www.nba.com/history/players/olajuwon_summary.html (November 2003)

O'Neal, Shaquille

Shaquille O'Neal (1972–), basketball player, was born in Newark, New Jersey. His father, a sergeant in the U.S. Army, was transferred to a base in West Germany when Shaquille was 10. There, the family lived on the military base. When Shaquille returned to America in 1987, he was almost 7 feet tall and a very good basketball player. In his two years at Cole High School in San Antonio, Texas, O'Neal led his team to a 68–1 record and a state title in his senior year. In three years at Louisiana State University (LSU), Shaq averaged 21.6 points and 13.5 rebounds a game. He led the nation in average rebounds per game (14.7) in 1991 and in average blocked shots per game (5.2) in 1992. A two-time All-American, he left college after his junior year. Shaquille O'Neal was chosen first in the 1992 National Basketball Association (NBA) draft and became an All-Star center with the Orlando Magic. O'Neal joined the Los Angeles Lakers for the 1996–97 season. He was the NBA Finals MVP for three consecutive seasons (2000–2002) as the Lakers captured the NBA Championship all three seasons. Shaquille O'Neal was voted as one of the NBA's 50 Greatest Players of All-Time.

Shaq Attack! His two mighty hands grabbed the ball as it bounced wildly off the defensive glass.

He turned, whipped a pass to a guard, and then sprinted down the middle of the court. Despite his huge size, Shaquille O'Neal ran with the ease of a little man.

As he reached the other end of the floor, the play developed with lightning speed. Shaq leaped toward the basket from just inside the foul line. A teammate lofted a pass high above the rim. In one explosive movement, the big man snatched the ball from the air and slammed it through the hole. In this brief period of a few seconds, Shaquille had made a statement that everyone in the arena understood.

Shaq slams the ball during a game against the Utah Jazz. The powerful Lakers center has shattered backboards and torn down baskets with his thunderous dunks.

O'Neal battles Duke's Christian Laettner for a rebound.

O'Neal, Shaquille

"When I get on the court," Shaq once explained, "I own it. I say to myself, 'This is my house, my paint, my ball.' I try to dominate."

Early Life

Shaquille Rashaun O'Neal was born on March 6, 1972, in Newark, New Jersey. His parents were members of Islam, a religion that began in the Arab world. In Arabic, their son's first two names together mean "little warrior." Shaquille was their first child. Two sisters and a brother followed.

Career Highlights

Two-time All-American selection at Louisiana State University (1991, 1992)

First player selected in the 1992 NBA Draft

Named 1993 NBA Rookie of the Year

Helped the Los Angeles Lakers win three straight NBA titles

Named NBA Finals MVP three time (2000, 2001, 2002)

Named one of the NBA's 50 Greatest Players of All-time

Shaquille's father was a soldier in the U.S. Army, and for many years he was stationed in New Jersey. Shaquille grew up there and at other Army bases around the world. When he was 10 years old, his father was transferred to a base in West Germany. (From 1949 until 1990, Germany had been divided into two separate countries—East Germany and West Germany.) Shaquille spent his early teenage years in West Germany, living on the base and attending school with other American kids.

Shaquille was a big kid. That was to be expected since both his parents stood over 6 feet tall. But tallness didn't make him great at sports. Classmates teased him about his size and his name. Shaquille was the class clown—and he got into a lot of trouble.

"In junior high in Germany," he recalled, "I fought kids all the time. I had a bad temper; I almost got thrown out of school."

By age 13, Shaquille had grown to be 6 feet, 5 inches, and he wore size 17 shoes. Who could blame a visiting college coach from the United States for mistaking Shaq for a full-grown man? When Shaquille asked coach Dale Brown how he could improve his jumping ability, the coach asked back in a friendly way, "How long have you been in the Army, soldier?"

"I'm not in the Army," said Shaq with a smile. "I'm only 13."

Shocked but delighted, the coach asked to speak to Shaquille's father. A few years later, Coach Brown had Shaq on his team.

A Dunk at 13

Not long after that meeting, Shaquille accomplished what most 13-year-olds only dream about—he dunked the ball. "It was a weak dunk," he remembered, "but I was like, 'Man, I just dunked.' I went to tell everybody and they wouldn't believe me, because I had bad knees and couldn't jump over a pencil."

Shaquille began spending more and more time working on his game. His heroes were Michael Jordan and Julius Erving—the great "Dr. J." His father noticed that Shaquille was trying too much to copy the Doctor's moves. "Son, being Dr. J is good, but you can't be Dr. J," he said to Shaquille.

After receiving a pass from teammate Scott Skiles (number 4) Shaq finishes the fast break in style.

"There's only one Dr. J. You want to be yourself."

Despite his father's advice, Shaquille had a hard time accepting who he was. He was so embarrassed about his large size that he tended to slouch. "My parents told me to be proud, but I wasn't," he recalled. "I wanted to be normal."

Things started to come together for Shaquille when he was about 15. He was gaining more coordination and more confidence. By the time his family moved back to the United States in 1987, Shaquille was ready to be a leader on a great high school basketball team.

At Cole High School in San Antonio, Texas, Shaquille led his team to a 68–1 record as a junior and senior. In his final year, the team went undefeated and took the Texas state championship.

By then, coaches throughout the country could see that O'Neal would be a great college center. Shaquille chose to attend Louisiana State University (LSU), mainly because the coach was Dale Brown, the man Shaq had met in Germany six years before.

Shaquille's years at LSU made him one of the most admired players in the country. In his sophomore season, he led the nation in rebounding with 14.7 rebounds a game, and he averaged 27.6 points per game. The next season, his 5.2 blocks per game placed him first among all college players.

His power impressed all who saw him play. In one game at LSU, Shaquille dunked the ball so hard that the whole support structure of the basket jumped five inches at the base, breaking the chain that anchored it to the floor. During his three years as a college player, Shaq slammed home 299 dunks—more than three a game. "I don't know what he's still doing

"I'm not satisfied with three [championship] rings. I want my five. Five is my goal. Then maybe I'd like to have six. Me and Lance [Armstrong]."

—Shaquille O'Neal, quoted in Sports Illustrated *in 2003*

in college," muttered one opposing center.

Many others had the same thought. After two years being named an All-American, Shaquille O'Neal decided to turn pro. In the 1992 National Basketball Association (NBA) draft, he was the first pick among all the players. The team that chose him was the Orlando Magic, which sorely needed a good player to help them rise in the standings.

Shaq backs in against Yao during a 2004 game. The All-Star centers have developed a friendly rivalry.

Turning Pro

At 7 feet, 1 inch, and about 300 pounds, Shaq had the size to dominate a game—even in the NBA. Yet, despite that size, he could move like a much smaller man. Even as a rookie, he was being compared to the greatest centers of all time, including Wilt Chamberlain, Kareem Abdul-Jabbar, and Bill Walton.

Both Kareem and Walton had spent time coaching Shaq as a college player. Kareem warned against comparisons. "Let him be the first Shaquille," said the NBA's all-time leading scorer.

Shaquille O'Neal made his mark quickly in the NBA. During a game in his first season, Shaq actually collapsed the entire backboard and support structure with one of his powerful dunks—it landed on top of the monster center. He was the only rookie ever named NBA Player of the Week in his first week of play. In only his fourth game, Shaq poured in 31 points, grabbed 21 rebounds, and blocked 4 shots as Orlando routed Washington.

With O'Neal in the center, the Magic had suddenly become one of the better NBA teams. And fans of Orlando looked forward to years of the fearsome Shaq Attack. Other players in the NBA knew that Shaq would soon become one of the best of all time. "He'll be great, and I mean great," said Magic

Shaquille O'Neal exploded onto the NBA scene in his rookie year. That season, 1992–93, he was chosen to play in the annual All-Star Game. Few expected the big center to make such an impact so quickly.

Johnson. "The guy's a monster—a true prime-time player."

Off to Los Angeles

Shaquille O'Neal joined the Los Angeles Lakers for the 1996–97 season and made the Lakers a contender again. Teaming with the young Kobe Bryant, the two players formed a fantastic duo. O'Neal emerged as a devastating monster, physically dominating hapless opponents. O'Neal, a perennial All-Star, finally achieved his dream in the 1999–2000 season when the Lakers won the NBA Championship. Shaq played like a star, earning the NBA Finals MVP. He also won the regular season MVP after averaging 29.7 points per game.

The Lakers repeated as NBA Champions the following two seasons, labeling them as one of the greatest teams ever. Although Kobe Bryant received a large part of the spotlight, there was no question that Shaq was the key to the Lakers' success.

Further Study

Smith, Pohla and Steve Wilson. *Shaquille O'Neal: Superhero at Center.* New York, NY: Rosen Publishing Group, 2003.

Stout, Glenn. *On the Court With Shaquille O'Neal.* New York, NY: Little, Brown, 2003.

Ungs, Tim. *Shaquille O'Neal.* New York, NY: Chelsea House Publishers, 1996.

O'Neil, Kitty

Kitty O'Neil (1948–), land-speed racer, was born in Corpus Christi, Texas. Though deaf since birth, Kitty did not let that interfere with her interest in sports. She moved to Wichita Falls, Texas, as a youngster and attended her mother's "School of Listening Eyes" for deaf students. As a teenager, Kitty moved with her family to Anaheim, California, where she pursued a diving career. Coached by former Olympic champion Sammy Lee, she won the Amateur Athletic Union (AAU) Junior Olympic diving title. In 1965, she was a diver on the U.S. Pan American Games team. After attending Fullerton (California) Junior College, O'Neil turned her attention to speed waterskiing. In 1970, she set a women's speed waterskiing record of 104.85 miles per hour. The highlight of Kitty O'Neil's sports career came in 1976, when she set a women's land-speed driving record of 512.710 miles per hour at the Alvord Desert in southeast Oregon. A year later, she set world speed and acceleration records for jet-powered vehicles. Kitty was also a stuntwoman.

Being deaf is not a handicap for Kitty Linn O'Neil. Her deafness has helped spur her to greatness in competition as a platform diver, a speed waterskier, a land-speed driver, and a Hollywood stuntwoman.

Part Irish and half Cherokee, Kitty was born deaf on March 24, 1948, in Corpus Christi, Texas. When she was very young, her family moved to Wichita Falls, Texas. There, Kitty learned to read lips at her mother's "School of Listening Eyes." Kitty entered regular school as a third-grader and was able to adjust easily. She later graduated from high school and went to Fullerton (California) Junior College.

Kitty took up sports at a young age. She was a fine swimmer and diver in her early teens. She was so good in diving that one year she entered the Amateur Athletic Union (AAU) Junior Olympics and won the diving competition.

Kitty O'Neil established the women's land-speed record of 512.710 miles per hour in 1976.

ROMATEC
RESEARCH LAB

"I just love danger. The feeling I get is just fantastic. It is a challenge to conquer, similar to being called on to do a difficult stunt."
—Kitty O'Neil

O'Neil, Kitty

Kitty had her heart set on making the U.S. diving team to compete in the Olympic Games at Tokyo, Japan, in 1964. She had transferred to a high school in Anaheim, California, so that she could be coached by former Olympic champion Sammy Lee. But a broken wrist and an attack of spinal meningitis prevented her from trying out for the 10-meter platform squad. But a year later she was selected as a member of the U.S. team in the Pan American Games.

After the Pan American Games, Kitty turned her interest to water skiing. In 1970, she set a speed-skiing record for women by traveling 104.85 miles per hour (mph).

That same year, she met Duffy Hambleton, a Hollywood stuntman, while she was racing motorcycles in cross-country events. They were later married. Kitty became a housewife in Southern California, but she yearned for the action that sports provided. So Duffy taught her some of the fine points of doing stunts.

In March 1976, Kitty joined some of the best daredevils in a cooperative association called Stunts Unlimited. Among her stunt assignments were hanging out of a six-story window, being set on fire in a graveyard, and attempting to get out of a sinking jet airliner.

After careful preparation, Kitty performs a fire stunt.

Winning Recognition

It is ironic that despite all her accomplishments, Kitty was hardly noticed until December 1976. Then, she announced that she would try to break the world land-speed record.

The record had been rising since the famed Sir Henry Seagrave became the first to exceed 200 mph in 1927. American Craig Breedlove became famous in the 1960s for pushing that record past 600 mph. In 1970, Gary Gabelich set a record of 620.407 mph on Utah's Bonneville Salt Flats.

Before her announcement, the 5-foot, 3-inch, 97-pound O'Neil had met car owner Bill Fredrick. He had designed and built a hydrogen-peroxide-fueled land-speed car called Motivator. The cockpit of the car was small. Kitty had to lie almost flat, with her head not much higher than her feet. Before she began practicing for the run at the Alvord Desert in southeast Oregon, Kitty had never driven a car like Motivator. But she adjusted to the lightweight machine quickly.

In the first trial, O'Neil did 300 mph effortlessly. She did 300 mph again the next day and 400 mph the third day. Her all-out attempt was planned for the fourth day, December 6.

As she took off for the record on the one-kilometer (.6-mile) course, she was up to 180 mph in five seconds, and over 500 mph in 15 seconds. Kitty hit a top speed of 618.340 mph and averaged

Kitty poses before climbing into the cockpit of a water-speed racer.

514.120 mph. In land-speed racing, international rules require the driver to make a return run in the opposite direction over the same one-kilometer course. In about an hour, Kitty drove the second run in almost exactly the same speed. Her average speed for both runs was 512.710 mph—about 200 mph faster than any woman had ever driven.

Kitty had used only about 60 percent of the Motivator's power. The day after she set the women's land-speed record, Kitty wanted to go for the men's record. But contract difficulties prevented her from doing so.

Career Highlights

Won the AAU Junior Olympic diving title in 1965

Member of the 1965 U.S. Pan-American Games team

Set a women's speed-skiing record in 1970 with a speed of 104.85 miles per hour

In 1976, travelled 512.710 mph, setting a women's land-speed driving record

New Challenges

After setting the record, Kitty O'Neil began to think of a few other stunts—like driving a jet-powered snowmobile, skiing behind a hydrogen-peroxide–fueled boat, and driving a piston-driven airplane.

In 1977, she set world speed and acceleration records for jet-powered vehicles. Driving at El Mirage Dry Lake in California, she was clocked at 392.54 mph over a quarter-mile course. She had a top terminal speed of 412 mph over a 500-meter course.

"I just love danger," Kitty has said. "The feeling I get is just fantastic. It is a challenge to conquer, similar to being called on to do a difficult stunt."

The fact that she was deaf did not deter her. In fact, Kitty said it may have helped her. "I'm able to concentrate 100 percent," she explained. "That helps me tremendously. If there were some way I could be made to hear, I wouldn't be interested. Why mess up a good thing?"

Husband Duffy agreed. "She has the asset of being able to totally shut off the outside world," he said. "On top of that, she is a great driver with an unusual ability. I have no doubt she will accomplish whatever she sets out to do."

Further Study

BOOKS

Garnder, Sandra. *Six Who Dared.* New York, NY: Messner, 1981.

Orr, Bobby

Bobby Orr (1948–), hockey player, was born in Parry Sound, Ontario, Canada. At 14, he became a member of the Oshawa Generals, a Junior "A" team. In his first season with the Boston Bruins of the National Hockey League (NHL), Orr received the Calder Trophy as the 1966–67 rookie of the year. In his second year in the NHL, he won the James Norris Trophy as the league's outstanding defenseman. Orr won that award eight straight seasons through 1974–75. From the 1969–70 through 1971–72 seasons, he received the Hart Trophy as the NHL's most valuable player. Twice, in 1969–70 and in 1974–75, he won the Art Ross Trophy as the league's leading scorer. Orr led the Boston Bruins to Stanley Cup victories in 1970 and 1972. He received the Conn Smythe Trophy as the most valuable player in the playoffs both years. In the 1970–71 season, he collected 102 assists, an NHL record. Orr signed with the Chicago Black Hawks in 1976, but chronic knee problems eventually forced him to retire. In 1979, 31-year-old Bobby Orr became the youngest man ever to be inducted into the Hockey Hall of Fame.

No player in hockey history had a greater impact on the game than Bobby Orr—known during the days he played with the Boston Bruins as "Mr. Hockey."

Legendary figures like Maurice Richard, Doug Harvey, Jean Beliveau, Gordie Howe, and Bobby Hull all became top box-office attractions during their brilliant careers. But not one of those great stars surpasses Orr, a magician on ice who is considered one of the best hockey players ever to lace up skates.

As a defenseman, Orr broke every record imaginable—and even set some marks that were thought to be impossible.

With his tremendous skating ability, Orr (number 4) was able to dominate play on the ice.

Orr, Bobby

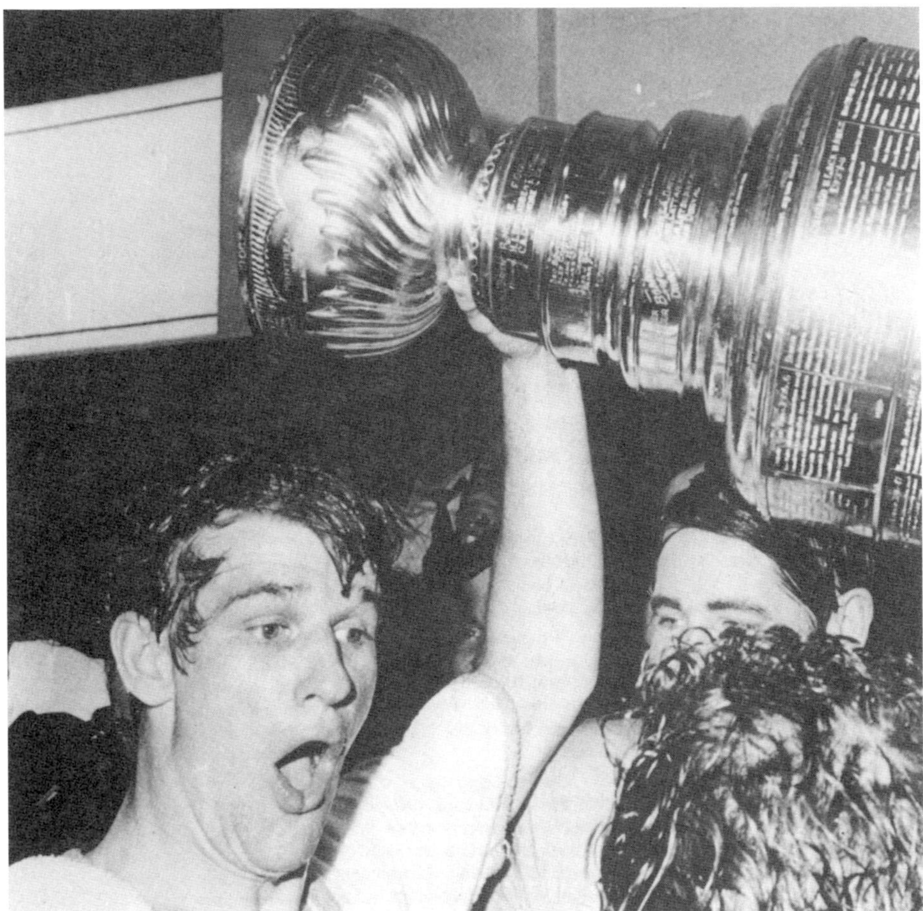

The locker room of the new champions was a happy place as Bobby whoops it up after he scored the winning goal that gave the Bruins the 1970 Stanley Cup. Orr holds up the giant Cup that he and his teammates fought so long to win.

Orr was a fluid, graceful skater. Often he practiced figure-eights at center ice while protecting his team's lead.

But Bobby Orr did much more than skate. He had a deadly accurate slap shot that exploded toward opposing goalies at speeds close to 100 miles per hour. When he shot from close range, Orr was equally deadly with his wrist shot.

With these two great talents—skating and shooting—Bobby Orr became the highest-scoring defenseman ever, and one of the top point-getters in the National Hockey League (NHL). In 1970–71, Orr went on a point-scoring spree. He scored 37 goals and 102 assists for 139 points (as of 2003 the most points by a defenseman in one season).

In Bobby Orr's brief but remarkable career, he won the Calder Memorial Trophy as the rookie of the year in the NHL (1966–67); the James Norris Memorial Trophy for the best defenseman eight straight years (1967–68 through 1974–75); the Hart Memorial Trophy as the league's most valuable player three straight seasons (1969–70 through 1971–72); the Art Ross Trophy as the NHL's leading scorer twice (1969–70 and 1974–75); and the Conn Smythe Trophy as the most valuable player in the playoffs two times (1970 and 1972). He also was selected to the NHL All-Star first team eight years in a row.

Early Life

Robert Gordon Orr was born in Parry Sound, Ontario, Canada, on March 20, 1948. As a youth, the future hockey star was on the ice learning how to skate. "I had him out there skating by the time he was three," remembered Bobby's father, Doug Orr. "He was always

"He was so dominant. Bobby was the greatest defenseman who ever played the game as far as I'm concerned. I believe in my heart he changed the face of the game."

—Phil Esposito

Orr comes to a screeching halt in front of the Philadelphia goal after he tried to take a pass from teammate Phil Esposito. Goalie Michel Belhumeur stopped the puck but caught a faceful of spray from Orr's skates.

falling down but he never stayed down. Even then he was fighting to get back on his feet so he could fall down again."

As the days went by, Bobby did not fall down as much. Soon he was winging around the pond with the older kids. Bobby had natural skating talent. He could play hockey with kids five and six years older than he was.

The Orrs were a close-knit family. Bobby's mother and father and brothers and sisters always came out to watch his games. By the time Bobby was 16, he was the best schoolboy player in Canada.

When Bobby was only 14, he commuted to Oshawa, 115 miles away. He played with the Oshawa Generals of the Junior "A" Ontario Hockey Association. Bobby played on the team with youngsters twice his size, but he held his own.

Striving To Succeed

With the great publicity he was getting, it would have been easy for Bobby to become too self-satisfied. But he did not. With the help of Generals' coach Wren Blair, Orr worked hard to improve his game. He wanted to become an even better player than the one the sportswriters were writing about.

Orr did get better. But he had to wait until he was 18 to play in the NHL. Then, in September 1966, Bobby Orr joined the Boston Bruins for his first season as a pro.

Orr, Bobby

Rookie Bobby Orr scored 13 goals and added 28 assists for 41 points. He also picked up 102 penalty minutes. He was involved in several fights with roughnecks who wanted to test the rookie's courage. They found out that Orr was very tough, and his desire to win could not be scared out of him. The Bruins had been a losing team when Orr arrived. But the team began to jell behind the aggressive playing of the multi-talented rookie.

Career Highlights

Won the 1966–67 Calder Trophy as the NHL rookie of the year

Won the James Norris Trophy (best defenseman) eight times during his career

Led the Boston Bruins to two Stanley Cup titles in 1970 and 1972

Named to the NHL All-Star first team eight times

Received the Hart Trophy as NHL Most Valuable Player three straight seasons (1970–72)

Youngest man to be elected to the Hockey Hall of Fame (31)

Bobby Orr gives a helping hand to Paula Pfeifer, the 1973 March of Dimes Poster Child. He took time from a practice session to help the charity start its new fund-raising drive.

In 1967–68, Orr played only 46 games because of an injury. But he still scored 11 goals and collected 20 assists. He won his first Norris Trophy as the NHL's best defenseman, and he led his team into the Stanley Cup playoffs.

An Awe-Inspiring Athlete

Crowds came to see Bobby Orr play. Expansion had spread new NHL teams across the United States and Canada. Some spectators were seeing hockey for the first time. They liked what they saw, especially when it was the Boston Bruins with Bobby Orr.

In 1968–69, Orr scored 21 goals and had 43 assists and took the Bruins to the Stanley Cup playoffs. The Bruins were beaten in the semifinals, but they had shown that they were an NHL powerhouse.

The fire that lit the Bruin keg of dynamite was Bobby Orr. In 1969–70, he had an amazing season. His 87 assists and his 120 points were the best in the NHL. In 14 playoff games, Orr scored nine goals and had 11 assists. He scored the winning goal in sudden-death overtime in the final game. Boston won its first Stanley Cup in 29 years.

Orr's sensational performance in the following season ended in disappointment. Orr tallied 37 goals and made 102 assists for 139 points. But the Bruins were eliminated in the quarter finals of the Stanley Cup.

In 1971–72, Boston came back and took the Cup for the second time in three years. They downed the New York Rangers in the sixth game of the final series.

Finding himself in a pack of New York Rangers, Orr (number 4) takes a shot on their goal.

Held Back by Injury

In the fall of 1972, Bobby Orr was named to Team Canada for its international series against the Soviet Union. (The Soviet Union broke apart into 15 states in 1991.) But knee surgery kept him out of action. He missed the beginning of the 1972–73 season, but he came on strong in the second half. He wound up with 29 goals and 72 assists for 101 points.

The next season, 1973–74, was another great one for Orr. He collected 32 goals and a league-leading 90 assists for 122 points. It was enough to take the Bruins to the finals of the playoffs, but they were defeated by the Philadelphia Flyers.

In 1974–75, he again led the league in assists with 89. He also took the Ross Trophy for the most points with 135. It was a record-setting sixth year in a row he had scored over 100 points. For the eighth straight year, Orr made the NHL All-Star first team. He was again awarded the Norris Trophy as the outstanding defenseman.

Harry Howell of the New York Rangers spoke for many players and coaches when he said, "Only one great hockey player comes along every 10 or 20 years, and Orr is that man for these 10 years."

Bobby Orr's knees failed him again. He played only 10 games in 1975–76. The Bruins were afraid he might never play again and refused to meet Orr's salary demands. His contract with Boston ended, and Bobby signed a five-year agreement with the Chicago Black Hawks.

But his knees could not take the strain. Orr spent most of the time as an assistant coach for the Black Hawks. Doctors had advised Orr that if he did not stop playing, he might be permanently crippled. He was eventually forced into retirement. In 657 career games, Orr had 270 goals and 645 assists.

In 1979, Bobby Orr became the youngest man ever, at 31, to be inducted into the Hockey Hall of Fame. The honor came only months after his retirement. Later that year, he was named special assistant to the NHL president.

Further Study

BOOKS

Kramer, S.A. *Hockey's Greatest Players.* New York, NY: Random House, 1999.

MacInnis, Craig. *Remembering Bobby Orr: A Celebration.* Toronto, ON: Stoddart, 1999.

WEB SITES

"Legends of Hockey," *Hockey Hall of Fame and Museum.* Online at www.legendsofhockey.net/html/legendsplayer.htm (November 2003)

Owens, Jesse

Jesse (James Cleveland) Owens (1913–1980), track-and-field star, was born in Danville, Alabama. His family moved to Cleveland, Ohio, where Owens became a track standout at East Technical High School. In 1934, while a freshman at Ohio State University, Owens set the world indoor record in the broad jump and tied the record in the 60-yard dash. In 1935, at the Big Ten Track and Field Meet at Ann Arbor, Michigan, Owens performed one of the greatest feats in sports history. In the span of 45 minutes, he set world records in the broad jump, the 220-yard dash, and the 220-yard low hurdles, and tied the world mark in the 100-yard dash. Owens competed at the Berlin Olympics in 1936 and once again was phenomenal. He won the broad jump and the 100- and 200-meter dashes. Jesse also ran one leg for the winning U.S. 400-meter relay team. He had captured four gold medals and had set three Olympic records. In 1976, Jesse Owens was awarded the Medal of Freedom by President Gerald R. Ford.

The annual Big Ten Track and Field Meet at Ann Arbor, Michigan, in 1935 drew a crowd of nearly 10,000 people. The fans expected to see some great performances. But there was a question whether Ohio State University's brilliant sophomore, Jesse Owens, would be able to compete. A week before the meet, Owens had hurt his back in a fall down a flight of stairs.

Owens was scheduled to compete in four events—the 100-yard dash, the 220-yard dash, the broad jump, and the 220-yard low hurdles. On the day of the meet, he soaked for an hour and a half in a tub of hot water to loosen his back muscles. And though he could barely bend over, he suited up for the meet.

In Chicago in 1936, Owens is shown winning the broad-jump competition during the NCAA meet. Owens also captured the 100-meter and 200-meter dashes and the 220-yard low hurdles.

158

Owens, Jesse

At the U.S. Interscholastic Track Meet in 1933, Owen (right) breaks the tape in the 220-yard dash in 20.7 seconds.

"I persuaded Larry [Snyder], my coach, to at least let me try the 100, and if I didn't do well in the finals, then we would withdraw from the rest of the races," Owens recalled.

Owens faced good competition in the 100-yard dash. But he concentrated more on not hurting his back than on his competitors or the official clocking. All four timers caught him at slightly over 9.3 seconds, giving him an official time of 9.4. Owens had tied the world record.

It was 3:15 p.m. when Jesse ran his brilliant 100. At 3:25 p.m. he lined up for his first attempt in the broad jump. Because a good jump was expected, a new pit had been built closer to the stands at the University of Michigan's Ferry Field. The new structure had a grass runway, which was considered too slippery for an outstanding leap. Ohio State's Coach Snyder complained bitterly about the runway.

Jesse Owens calmly placed a handkerchief at 26 feet, 2½ inches, the world record distance. Owens then jumped 26 feet, 8¼ inches on his first attempt. That

"It dawned on me with blinding brightness. I realized: I had jumped into another rare kind of stratosphere—one that only a handful of people in every generation are lucky enough to know."

—Jesse Owens, on his Olympic achievements

Far ahead of the field, Owens ties the world record in the 100-yard dash in 1935 with a time of 9.4 seconds.

world record was not beaten for 25 years.

At 3:34 p.m., Owens got into position for the 220-yard dash. Jesse streaked around the track in 20.3 seconds—15 yards ahead of the field. His time was three-tenths of a second faster than the world record.

At 4:00 p.m., Owens was at the starting line again, this time for the 220-yard low hurdles, which is seldom run anymore. His clocking for this event was 22.6 seconds—four-tenths of a second faster than the world record.

In a 45-minute span, Jesse Owens had set three world records and tied another. No man in the history of track has ever done as well, before or since.

That superhuman effort was typical of Owens. His amateur career lasted only through high school, two years of college, and the 1936 Olympic Games. During those few years, he smashed record after record. Then Owens turned professional to capitalize on his fame. He continued to be a success—on and off the track.

J. C. Becomes Jesse

James Cleveland Owens was born on September 12, 1913, in Danville, Alabama. He was one of eight children. To help feed the family, young J. C., as his family called him, had to pick cotton when he was only six. The Owens family moved north to Cleveland, Ohio, to seek a better living.

In Cleveland, J. C. Owens attended junior high school. He had not lost his Alabama accent. When his teacher asked his name, he said "J. C." But the teacher thought he said "Jesse." Too shy to correct her, J. C. was "Jesse" from then on.

When the young Southern boy first ran in a junior high school track practice, the coach looked in amazement at the time on his stopwatch. He checked the watch to see if it was running too slowly. It seemed impossible for anyone young and untrained to move so fast. But the watch was right.

Owens, Jesse

Soaring through the air, Owens captures the Olympic broad jump in 1936 with a record leap of 26 feet, 5¼ inches.

Winning Recognition

During his years at Cleveland's East Technical High School, Jesse Owens became nationally known.

He tied world records in the dashes, and he took the national championship in the broad jump. At a national high school track meet in Chicago during Jesse's senior year, he won the 100-yard dash in 9.4, the 220-yard dash in 20.7, and the broad jump with a leap of 24 feet, 9½ inches.

After graduation, he went to Ohio State University in Columbus. Since he had no scholarship, he had to work full time. There was little time left after classes, work, and track practice. Yet Jesse continued to work, and he did very well academically. His great athletic performance continued.

Coach Larry Snyder knew he had a prize catch in Jesse Owens. But he also knew that Owens had not yet reached his full potential. As a runner, Owens's arm action was too short. In the broad jump, he did not start correctly, and his jump was not smooth. The young athlete also needed to work on his dash starts, and he needed to build up his endurance.

Polishing His Game

He worked hard and, under Snyder's guidance, he began to perfect his skills. Early in his first collegiate season (1934), Owens set a world indoor record in the broad jump. And he tied the world indoor mark in the 60-yard dash. Outdoors, he won the national Amateur Athletic Union (AAU) title in the broad jump.

When he was a sophomore, Jesse Owens set a new indoor mark with the first 6.1-second clocking in the 60-yard dash. This also was the year of his fantastic performance at the Big Ten meet in Ann Arbor, where he broke three world records and tied a fourth. At the National Collegiate Athletic Association (NCAA) meet in Berkeley, California, Owens won four individual titles. No other athlete had ever won more than two.

Young admirers wait patiently for autographs from Ohio State track star Jesse Owens at the NCAA meet in Chicago in 1936.

Owens, Jesse

His next great challenge came the following year.

An Historic Event

The 1936 Olympics held in Berlin, Germany, are sometimes called the "Hitler Olympics."

The Nazi dictator, Adolph Hitler, wanted the Games to be a showcase for the dominance of the German "Aryan" peoples. Hitler expected Germany to win athletically and then politically. He repeatedly told his countrymen that they were the superior race, and that blacks and Jews were inferior.

A German soldier watches as Owens (center) completes an autograph for him at the 1936 Olympics.

Career Highlights

Set world indoor record for broad jump and tied record for 60-yard dash while a freshman in college

Set or tied four world record in a one-hour span during 1935 Big Ten Track and Field Meet

Won four gold medals at 1936 Olympics in Berlin, Germany

Set three Olympic records at 1936 Olympics

Awarded Medal of Freedom in 1976

But if one man upset Hitler's grand design for the Olympics, it was Jesse Owens—the grandson of an American slave. Before Owens finished competing in the Berlin Games, even the German spectators cheered for him.

Jesse won the 100-meter dash, the 200-meter dash, and the broad jump. Then he ran a leg for the winning U.S. 400-meter relay team. In each contest, he set an Olympic record. But his 10.3-second record in the 100 meters was scratched because of a slight following wind.

Jesse Owens received four gold medals. He was the first American athlete in the history of Olympic track-and-field competition to do so.

Before Owens was handed his fourth gold medal on the victory stand, Hitler had stomped out of the stadium.

Jesse Owens was a national hero. "He was at his best in the big meets," his coach said later. "He won eight Big Ten championships, eight NCAA championships, and four Olympic gold medals. But he also typified everything that a great man must possess."

Jesse Owens left college before his senior year and turned professional. Times had been hard

Wearing the victory laurels, Owens (center) salutes the American flag during the playing of the national anthem at the 1936 Olympics. His gold-medal-winning leap in the broad jump established an Olympic record.

for the Owens family, and the opportunity to earn some money was at hand.

Besides, there were few worlds left for Owens to conquer in amateur track. He had set world records in seven events, unofficial records in two events, and records in three indoor events. He was unbeaten in college outdoor competition. His world long-jump record was not broken for 25 years, and his Olympic long-jump record lasted 24 years.

Owens continued to run in professional exhibitions until 1948. He also became effective at public speaking and public relations.

In 1976, President Gerald R. Ford awarded Jesse Owens the Medal of Freedom, the highest honor the United States can bestow on a civilian.

Further Study

BOOKS

McKissack, Patricia and Fredrick. *Jesse Owens: Olympic Star.* Berkeley Heights, NJ: Enslow Publishers, 2001.

Nuwer, Hank. *The Legend of Jesse Owens.* New York, NY: F. Watts, 1998.

Streissguth, Tom. *Jesse Owens.* Minneapolis, MN: Lerner Publications, 1999.

WEB SITES

Jesse Owens: The Official Website. Online at www.jesseowens.com/ (November 2003)

Paige, Satchel

Satchel (LeRoy) Paige (1905–1982), baseball player, was born in Mobile, Alabama. He signed his first professional contract in 1926 with the Chattanooga Lookouts, one of the old barnstorming Negro League teams. For the next 22 years, Paige was not only the most dominant but also the most colorful pitcher in the Negro Leagues. Statistics were rarely kept, but in the summer of 1933 Paige posted a 31–4 record with 16 shutouts and an average of 15.6 strikeouts per game. Known for his "rubber" arm, he pitched almost 125 games a year for over 20 years. The color line in baseball was broken in 1947, and Paige finally made it to the big leagues at the age of 43, long past his prime. He spent two years with the Cleveland Indians in 1948 and 1949, and three with the St. Louis Browns from 1951 through 1953, achieving only mild success. Paige pitched several more years against minor league competition before retiring in 1966 at the age of 61. He spent two years as a coach with the Atlanta Braves and was named to the Baseball Hall of Fame in 1971.

Many baseball historians insist that Satchel Paige was the greatest pitcher who ever lived, but his complete records are not found in the major league register. That is because Paige spent the majority of his playing days in the Negro Leagues. When the color barrier in major league baseball was finally broken in 1947, Paige was well past his prime.

Paige pitched effectively with the Cleveland Indians and the St. Louis Browns from 1948 through 1953. He helped the Indians to the pennant in 1948. Unfortunately, his break did not come until he was 43 years old.

Major leaguers who played

Pitching for the minor league Miami Marlins in 1956, Paige takes a rest while his team is at bat.

Paige, Satchel

Soon after signing with the Cleveland Indians in 1948, Paige demonstrates his stuff.

against Paige in barnstorming trips against the Negro League teams know that, as a pitcher, Paige was in a class by himself. Joe DiMaggio, Charlie Gehringer, Rogers Hornsby, Jimmie Foxx, and others batted against Paige and compared him to the best.

"He was the best I ever faced," DiMaggio stated. "After I got that [first] hit off him, I knew I was ready for the big leagues."

Paige also opposed the legendary pitcher Dizzy Dean 10 times and beat him on 6 occasions, including a 1–0 victory in 13 innings.

Negro League

It is estimated that Paige pitched in more than 2500 games in his lifetime. He claimed to have won 2000 of these games. Of these victories, Paige probably pitched about 250 shutouts, including nearly 100 no-hit games.

Satchel Paige pitched 22 years in the Negro Leagues. He pitched for many clubs; for some, he was practically a whole franchise. When he was in his prime, his drawing power was the difference between the success and failure of many clubs.

Paige signed with the Pittsburgh Crawfords, one of the best Negro League teams, in 1931. During the 1940s, Paige played for the Kansas City Monarchs, another top team.

No one knows for sure the records Paige compiled because accurate records were not kept in the Negro Leagues. For an idea of how good Paige was, take a look at his record for 1933, a year in which his statistics were charted. That summer, Paige posted a record of 31–4, with 16 of his victories coming on shutouts. He averaged 15.4 strikeouts per game.

Those who followed the Negro Leagues in the 1930s estimate that Paige pitched 125 games a year—both summer and winter—for about 20 years. Skipping from one team to another—nearly 250 teams between 1926 and 1948—he sometimes played for a team on a one-day basis. Sometimes he would pitch seven games in a week. One month in 1935, he pitched 29 days in a row while freelancing for Bismarck, North Dakota, in a semipro league. In the off-season, Paige barnstormed the country and also traveled to

"Age is a question of mind over matter. If you don't mind, it doesn't matter."

—Satchel Paige, on why he pitched until he was 61 years old

Mexico, Venezuela, Puerto Rico, and the Dominican Republic to play ball.

A Successful Showman

Satchel Paige dominated Negro League baseball. Wearing a uniform with either "Satchel" or "Paige" across his shirt, the pitcher played with any team that would pay $500 to $2000 for three innings of his work. (This would equal about $6,000 to $27,000 in 2003.) His travel average was 30,000 miles a year and his earnings in some years was $37,500 (equal to more than $500,000 in 2003). He was advertising himself as "Satchel Paige, world's greatest pitcher, guaranteed to strike out the first nine men."

A sinewy 6-foot, 4-inch, 190-pounder, Paige was said to have a "rubber arm." That means he could throw for days on end without tiring his arm. Paige claimed he never had a sore arm in his career. He worked in a easy, effortless fashion that produced no strain. He was his own masseur, and olive oil was the only lubricant he used. If his arm got stiff, he soaked it in an hour-long steam bath, using water as hot as he could stand.

In 1934, after pitching a no-hitter for the Pittsburgh Crawfords against the Homestead Grays in Pittsburgh, Paige drove all night to Chicago. There, he shut out the American Giants, 1–0, in 12 innings.

In 1958, at the age of 52, Satchel Paige threw 110 innings for the minor-league Miami Marlins and posted an earned-run average of 2.95.

A remarkable athlete, Paige was also a showman. His wind-up was exaggerated, and he would throw from every angle. He had a variety of pitches, including the "hesitation" pitch, a bewildering delivery in which Paige stopped in mid-throw before following through.

Bob Feller, who played with Paige for the Cleveland Indians, admitted he never saw a pitcher who could throw from so many angles and in so many styles as Paige.

"If I ever tried to throw the way Paige does, I'd wrench my arm out," explained Feller.

In his early years, Paige's best pitch was his fastball. By the time he got to the majors in 1948, he had become more of a curveball pitcher. His greatest asset was his control. He signed his first professional contract in 1926 with the Chattanooga Lookouts. The

Paige, Satchel

team's manager had just watched him knock 14 tin cans off a fence from the regulation pitching distance.

The Early Years

The year of Paige's birth was uncertain for many years. But in 1979, the Baseball Hall of Fame received the official record of his birth—July 7, 1905. Leroy Page (later changed to LeRoy Paige) was born in Mobile, Alabama, where he learned the art of pitching by throwing rocks at tin cans.

> ## *Career Highlights*
>
> Pitched 55 career no-hitters over 20 seasons in the Negro Leagues
>
> Posted a 31–4 record in 1933 with 16 shutouts
>
> Became the first African-American pitcher in the majors when he debuted with Cleveland in 1948 at age 42
>
> At age 59, started a 1965 game for Kansas City, striking out one and allowing only one hit over three innings
>
> Inducted into the Baseball Hall of Fame in 1971

This plaque in Cooperstown, New York, was installed when Paige was inducted into the Hall of Fame in 1971.

The origin of the nickname "Satchel" is also a mystery. Paige denied that it is short for "satchel foot," a name that would recognize his size 14 shoes. He said he got the name when he was about 7 years old. In order to provide his family with a little more money, he carried luggage at the railroad station in Mobile.

"Why, I carried so many satchels that all you could see was satchels," he explained. "You couldn't see no LeRoy Paige at all. So the kids started calling me 'Satchel' and it stuck."

Life in the Major League

One year after Jackie Robinson and the Brooklyn Dodgers had broken baseball's color barrier, Satchel Paige signed a contract with the Cleveland Indians under Bill Veeck.

Paige, a "rookie" at the age of 43, proved a valuable asset and a drawing card for the Indians. In his first three starts, he drew 201,829 fans, including 73,382 in Chicago. He won six games and lost one that first year, compiling a 2.47 earned-run average (ERA) and pitching two shutouts. He appeared in a World Series game, pitching two-thirds of an inning in relief.

Paige finished the 1949 season with a 4–7 record and a 3.04 ERA. When the Indians began a "youth movement" the following season, Paige and Veeck were left out.

After a year in the Negro Leagues, Paige returned in 1951 to work under Veeck with the St. Louis Browns. Paige had an off year with a 3–4 record and a 4.79 ERA, but he bounced back in 1952 to win 12 games and save 10 others. He was the best relief pitcher in the league. He compiled

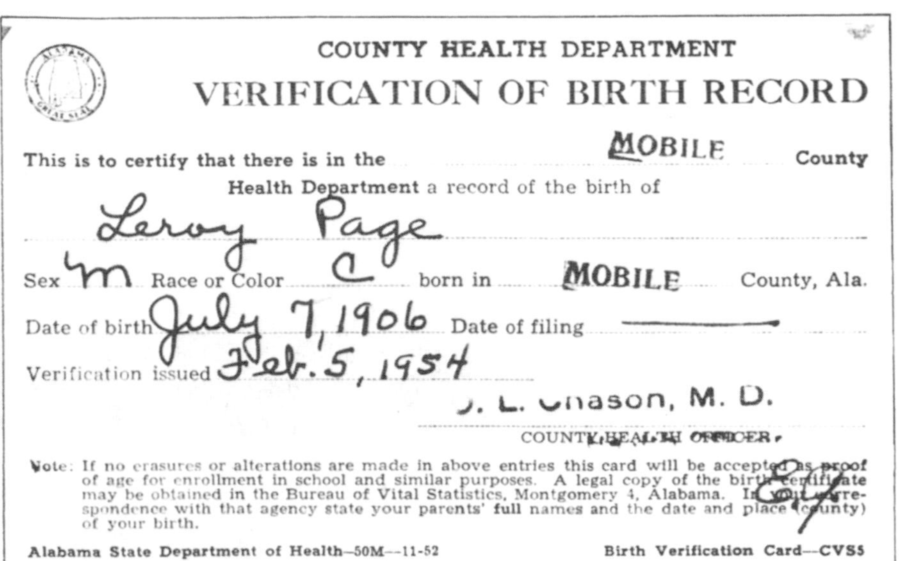

COUNTY HEALTH DEPARTMENT

VERIFICATION OF BIRTH RECORD

This is to certify that there is in the MOBILE County Health Department a record of the birth of

Leroy Page

Sex M Race or Color C born in MOBILE County, Ala.

Date of birth July 7, 1906 Date of filing ——

Verification issued Feb. 5, 1954

J. L. Chason, M. D.

COUNTY HEALTH OFFICER

Note: If no erasures or alterations are made in above entries this card will be accepted as proof of age for enrollment in school and similar purposes. A legal copy of the birth certificate may be obtained in the Bureau of Vital Statistics, Montgomery 4, Alabama. In your correspondence with that agency state your parents' full names and the date and place (county) of your birth.

Alabama State Department of Health—50M—11-52 Birth Verification Card—CVS5

The exact age of Satchel paige was always in doubt, and the former pitching star had great fun keeping people guessing. This "verification" lists Paige's date of birth as July 7, 1906.

a 3–9 record with a 3.54 ERA in 1953. At the end of that season, the Browns left St. Louis, Bill Veeck left the major leagues, and so did Paige.

Once more, Paige returned to the Negro Leagues, and then he faded into the minor leagues. In 1965, at the amazing age of 60, Satchel Paige returned to the majors for one game, pitching three scoreless innings for the Kansas City Athletics against the Boston Red Sox.

In 1968, he was signed as a coach for the Atlanta Braves and worked with them through the 1969 season.

Paige's Rules

During his playing career, Paige had adopted several rules on how to stay young. "These rules for staying young are mighty good for anybody," he declared.

Avoid fried meats which angry up the blood.

If your stomach disputes you, lie down and pacify it with cool thoughts.

Keep the juices flowing by jangling around gently as you move.

Go very light on the vices, such as carrying on in society—the social ramble ain't restful.

Avoid running at all times.

And don't look back. Something might be gaining on you.

"When you look back," Satch explained, "you know how long you've been going and that just might stop you from going any farther. And with me, there was an awful lot to look back on. So I didn't. That let me keep on going, and keeping going more than anything else made ol' Satch the reputation he had. That and a good fastball."

In 1971, Paige finally got the recognition that was denied him for all those years he spent in the Negro Leagues. That year, Satchel Paige was elected to the Baseball Hall of Fame by a committee chosen to honor former greats of the Negro Leagues.

His name now holds a permanent place on a plaque in the Hall of Fame at Cooperstown, New York. But somehow a place in the hallowed halls of the National Archives in Washington, D.C., seems more appropriate. Satchel Paige is, indeed, a special part of American folklore.

Further Study

BOOKS

McKissack, Patricia and Fredrick. *Satchel Paige: The Best Arm in Baseball.* Berkeley Heights, NJ: Enslow Publishers, 2002.

Schmidt, Julie. *Satchel Paige.* New York, NY: Rosen Central, 2002.

WEB SITES

Baseball Almanac. Online at www.baseball-almanac.com/players/ballplayer.shtml (November 2003).

"Satchel Paige" *National Baseball Hall of Fame.* Online at www.baseballhalloffame.org/hofers_and_honorees/hofer_bios/paige_satchel.htm (November 2003)

Palmer, Arnold

Arnold Palmer (1929–), golfer, was born near Latrobe, Pennsylvania. He began swinging sawed-off golf clubs at 3 and later started to take lessons from his father. Losing only one match in high school competition, Palmer was the state amateur champion five times. At Wake Forest College, Palmer was twice a national intercollegiate medalist. He later won the National Amateur championship in 1954. Arnold joined the pro tour in 1955. Soon, he became famous as an attractive and energetic personality who could come from far behind to win a tournament. Palmer ranks fourth to Sam Snead, Jack Nicklaus, and Ben Hogan in the number of tournament victories, with 60.

His major championships included four Masters titles (1958, 1960, 1962, and 1964), two British Opens (1961 and 1962), and one U.S. Open title (1960). He also played on five Ryder Cup teams and six winning World Cup teams. Later, Palmer was a star attraction on the Senior PGA Tour.

Arnold Palmer was the man who took pro golfers out of station wagons and put them into jet airplanes, Until he began to dominate the professional tour in the early 1960s, the pros used to scrape for a living, crossing the country by car—"following the sun," as they said. There was little prestige, except for a handful of top golfers, and there was little prize money for any of them.

But Palmer came along in the 1950s, quickly established himself at the end of the decade, and boosted the sport in money and prestige in the 1960s.

Palmer and his followers, called "Arnie's Army," were the talk of the sports world in the 1960s. Golf went big time. Arnold Palmer was named the "Outstanding Athlete of the Decade—1960–69" by sportswriters and sportscasters across the country.

Palmer had a magic about him that enabled him to dominate the pro tour and become the sport's first millionaire. He was the friendly son of a greenskeeper

With a high finish on his follow through, Palmer watches the flight of his tee shot.

"I've always made a total effort, even when the odds seemed entirely against me. I never quit trying; I never felt that I didn't have a chance to win."

—Arnold Palmer

Palmer, Arnold

Mouths agape, Palmer and his gallery react as this bunker shot in the 1968 PGA Championship bounces in and out of the hole.

who broke through in a rich man's game. He became a millionaire at the game he made popular. By the time the 1960s ended, golf as a spectator sport had shot up in crowd appeal and television ratings. No person close to the golf world could deny that Palmer was the most important figure in that growth.

Learning a Gentleman's Game

His own growth as a golfer started at an early age. Born on September 10, 1929, near Latrobe, Pennsylvania, where he grew up, Palmer learned the game from his father. Young Arnold took his first swing with a club when he was 3 years old.

Through his father's coaching, Arnold began to master the game.

The two would go out on the course at Latrobe, where his father worked, on Mondays when it was closed to the members. By age 9, Palmer shot nine holes of golf for a 45 score.

He practiced consistently whenever he could. But there were other lessons to learn, too. Arnold once got mad after blowing a shot in an important amateur meet and he violently threw his club over a grove of trees. His dad heard about it and pulled him aside. As Arnold recalls the conference: "Pop told me this was a gentleman's game, and that he was ashamed of me. If he saw or heard of me throwing a club again, he was through with me as a golfer. That did it."

Palmer moved up fast in the western Pennsylvania golfing circles. As a high school freshman, he shot a 71. He was the star at Latrobe High, the state's best junior golfer for three years, and the state amateur champ five times.

Winning Recognition

His golf game attracted attention beyond the state borders, and Palmer was given a scholarship to attend Wake Forest College in North Carolina in 1947. He continued to star there, but he got restless and left school before he graduated. He joined the Coast Guard.

Palmer never lost interest in golf, though. After he got out of the service, he went back to school briefly, then took a sales job that enabled him to get out on the

At this banquet in 1970, Arnold Palmer was named "Athlete of the Decade" in a poll of sportswriters. Here he demonstrates his grip for his father, who was once his instructor.

course in the afternoons. In 1954, Palmer won the National Amateur title of the United States Golf Association. He was on the way to the stardom that he had desired for some time.

"Ever since I was big enough to dream I have wanted to be the best golfer that ever lived," he recalled later. The victory at the U.S. Amateur hinted that he had the makings of a star. He decided to go on the pro tour.

Married late in 1954, Palmer made some sacrifices to get himself on the road along with those other hopeful golfers who followed the sun. Arnold got rolling with a second-hand house trailer, which he bought after getting a $600 loan from his father. He was not quite ready for his first jet plane then, but success came fast. In 1958, he became pro golf's leading money-winner, taking home over $40,000 in prize money.

But men had made that kind of money before. Palmer set about on a course that would make him the most famous golfer ever in the next couple of years. Palmer became known for his unbelievable finishes. In 1960 alone, he rallied from way behind to win both the Masters and the U.S. Open championships.

A Stunning Success

At the Masters in Augusta, Georgia, Palmer went into the final two holes needing two birdies. He got the first on a 30-foot putt and the second with a 300-yard drive that landed on the green, a mere eight feet from the flag. He calmly putted the eight feet in one stroke.

Two months later at Denver, Arnold Palmer seemed about as likely a winner of the U.S. Open as the groundskeeper. He had completed the first three 18-hole rounds. There was just one remaining round to play. Palmer was in 13th place, seven strokes out of the lead.

Palmer studies a putt as fellow golfing great Jack Nicklaus leans over to offer some advice. They were members of the U.S. Ryder Cup team that defeated Great Britain in 1971.

Palmer, Arnold

At lunch before the final round, Arnold studied his chances, which were next to nothing. He asked his friends what would happen if he went out and shot a 65.

"Nothing," they said.

"Maybe so," said Palmer, "but let's shoot the 65 and see what happens."

He shot a stunning 30 for the first nine holes and the opponents began nervously to figure their own chances, even though some of them were still ahead of Palmer. Palmer shot an even-par 35 for the final nine holes—just enough to give him a one-shot victory. It was the greatest comeback in Open history.

Career Highlights

Pennsylvania Amateur Championship five times

1954 National Amateur Champion

Posted 60 career PGA tournament victories, fourth all-time

Won the Masters four times (1958, 1960, 1962, 1964)

Captured a total of seven major championships

Two-time PGA Player of Year (1960 and 1962)

Inducted into both the PGA Hall of Fame and International Golf Hall of Fame

Tied for the lead with Jack Nicklaus on the final hole of the 1970 Byron Nelson Classic, Palmer excitedly urges his putt toward the cup.

He continued to win the big ones—the Masters four times, the British Open twice, and the Ryder Cup and World Cup often with his American teammates.

Before long, Palmer unloaded his house trailer and began traveling by jet. He had organized a vast business network that included clothing companies, insurance businesses, putting greens, and several other interests. He was making as much off the course as he was on it, and both incomes were huge.

Palmer was making a million dollars a year or more on all his enterprises as the 1960s neared their end. Other golfers—such as Jack Nicklaus, Billy Casper, and Gary Player—began pushing him out of the first places, though Palmer hung onto his popularity.

But if anything could sum up how important he was to golf, it had to be the $128,855 he won in 1970 when he did not even win a tournament. Before Arnold Palmer put golf in the big money, that would not have been possible.

In a 1986 senior event, Palmer became the first touring pro to record holes-in-one on the same hole in successive days.

Further Study

BOOKS

Durbin, William. *Arnold Palmer.* Philadelphia, PA: Chelsea House Publishers, 1998.

Palmer, Arnold. *A Golfer's Life.* New York, NY: Ballantine Books, 1999.

WEB SITES

Arnold Palmer Enterprises: The Name Means Golf. Online at www.arnoldpalmer.com (November 2003)

Pastrana, Travis

Travis Pastrana (1983–), professional motorcyclist, was born October 8, 1983, in Annapolis, Maryland. Travis Pastrana learned to ride motorcycles competitively by the age of 8. By age 18, he was one of the top motocross performers in history. Pastrana is a five-time American Motorcyclist Association (AMA) Amateur National Champion. He is also the youngest rider ever to win a national championship as a professional. Pastrana is best known for the aerial tricks he has used to win numerous freestyle titles. In his short professional career, Pastrana has won four ESPN Summer X-Games gold medals and two Gravity Games gold medals in freestyle motocross.

Travis Pastrana, son of Robert and Debbie Pastrana, was born and raised in Annapolis, Maryland. When Travis was only 4 years old, his father bought him his first motorcycle, a one-speed Honda Z-50. Travis fell in love with motocross racing and began practicing the sport religiously. When he was 8 years old, he stormed to a second-place finish at the AMA Amateur Nationals. The high finish caught the attention of Suzuki, a motorcycle company that sponsors motocross racers. Travis became the youngest rider ever to join the Suzuki support team.

Motocross has been around for as long as there has been motorcycle racing. Modern motocross became popular in the late 1970s, but new technology has allowed the sport to evolve. There are three types of motocross: (1) traditional, (2) supercross, and (3) freestyle.

The main type of off-road motorcycle racing is traditional motocross. Traditional motocross entails outdoor track racing with hilly terrain that allows riders to perform tricks off of jumps.

Supercross, a variation of motocross, is usually performed indoors. Supercross tracks are smaller because of the indoor size limitations. Supercross focuses more on the precision of jumps.

Freestyle motocross is a newer event categorized as an extreme sport. Experience is critical to freestyle competition. In freestyle, riders perform radical jumping tricks high in the air. They are judged based on difficulty and creativity. This attention-grabbing form of motocross is most commonly seen in the X-Games (X stands for extreme) and Gravity Games.

Rising Star

From 1992 to 1999, Travis Pastrana won five AMA Amateur National Championships. During that

Travis Pastrana celebrates after landing a 360-degree backflip during the final round of the 2003 X Games Mot X freestyle finals in Los Angeles.

PUMA
PUMA

"I am truly living a dream by being able to ride a motorcycle for a living."
—Travis Pastrana

Pastrana, Travis

span, he also became the World Freestyle Champion in 1998. He was only 14 years old. During the summer of 1999, Pastrana solidified his hold as the best freestyler in the world when he won the Gravity Games gold medal in freestyle motocross. He proceeded to win two more gold medals at the ESPN Summer X-Games—one in singles and one in doubles.

He awed audiences with his high-flying tricks and became a celebrity by launching his motorcycle into the San Francisco Bay during the competition. He finished 1999 by earning the Horizon Award, given to the best amateur rider.

Pastrana was named the 2000 AMA Rookie of the Year after a spectacular campaign as a first-year professional. He emerged victorious as the AMA 125cc Outdoor National Champion in motocross (125cc refers to the size of the motorcycle engine). Pastrana also became the youngest rider ever to represent the United States in the *Motocross des Nations.* Team USA, led by Pastrana, secured victory. He ended his year by defending his X-Games championship, becoming the back-to-back freestyle motocross gold medalist.

The year 2001 was a roller coaster ride for Pastrana. He battled a series of injuries while capturing individual titles. He earned his third consecutive X-Games gold medal and finished atop the leader board at the Gravity Games. It was his second career Gravity Games gold medal in freestyle motocross. He also emerged as champion of the AMA 125cc Eastern Region Supercross Series.

Pastrana looked to repeat his 2000 performance as AMA Outdoor National Champion, but he suffered a series of three concussions from crashes. He was forced to sit out and watch someone else grab the title.

Looking back on his 2001 showing, Travis said, "I was able to win a supercross championship for the first time, but I suffered a lot of injuries. That's the way it goes in this sport...good breaks and bad breaks."

Tricky

While Travis Pastrana remains a top motocross racer, his performances in the freestyle venues are what make him a celebrity. Without question, Pastrana has revolutionized the freestyle scene. His acrobatic tricks and high-flying stunts thrill fans from coast to coast. By 2004, he had not lost a freestyle competition since its inception in 1998.

Much of his success can be attributed to his personal creativity. He said, "I can learn a new trick fairly quickly, and I am pretty creative when it comes to inventing new tricks. Freestyle is as much fun as racing but not as much work."

Pastrana is the creator of numerous tricks, including the Rodeo, Cliffhanger, and Lazy Boy. Many consider Pastrana's best trick the Kiss of Death Lookback, but his signature move is the One Hand Fender Grab Superman Indian Air. The trick is even more difficult to

Career Highlights

Five time National Amateur Champion

1998 World Freestyle Champion at age 14

Won four ESPN X-Games gold medals

Two-time Gravity Games gold medalist

Youngest rider ever to win a national championship in motocross

2000 American Motocross Association (AMA) Rookie of the Year

Travis Pastrana does a trick while competing in the freestyle motocross during the 2002 Gravity Games in Cleveland. Pastrana captured the gold medal.

perform than it is to say. While in mid-air, Pastrana scissor-kicks his legs straight back. He keeps one hand on the handlebars and grabs the rear fender of his motorcycle with his other hand. Pastrana routinely performs this dangerous maneuver to perfection, leaving the crowd amazed.

Fun and Games

As the most recognized athlete in motocross today, Travis Pastrana has reached star status. His name is included on toys and trading cards, and he has appeared in a series of instructional motocross videos. Much of the money Pastrana accumulates from his endorsements is used to purchase machinery and supplies and to build his own motocross track in the backyard of his Annapolis home.

Travis Pastrana never lived the ordinary teenage lifestyle. His motocross schedule was too hectic. Although he never got the chance to go to high school parties and dances, he did complete his high school education—almost three years ahead of schedule! Travis graduated from high school at age 15 with a 3.9 grade-point average and as a member of the Suzuki Good Scholars Program. He currently is continuing his education by taking Internet-based classes via the University of Maryland, where he is a straight-A student focusing on communications and English.

At a young age, Travis Pastrana has accomplished more than most people can dream of. He is a world champion in a sport that he cherishes. Pastrana said, "I just keep it fun and give it my all. How could I not keep going when I am making a living doing something I love?" Chances are good that motocross fans will continue to see Travis Pastrana tear up tracks for many years to come.

Further Study

J. Poolos. *Extreme Sports Biographies: Travis Pastrana.* New York: Rosen Publishing Group, 2004.

Payton, Walter

Walter Payton (1954–1999), football player, was born in Columbia, Mississippi. He attended Jackson State University, where he was an all-purpose star on the football team. As a collegian, he rushed for 3563 yards and scored a record 464 points. In 1975, Payton was drafted by the Chicago Bears of the National Football League (NFL). He gained 1852 yards rushing to lead the league in 1977. That year, he also set a single-game rushing record of 275 yards, which stood until September 2003. For his efforts, he was named the 1977 United Press International (UPI) Athlete of the Year. In 1984, Payton broke Jim Brown's all-time rushing record. He went on to set many other NFL marks. Twice, Walter won the Jim Thorpe Trophy as the league's most valuable player. Payton helped lead the Bears to victory in the 1986 Super Bowl. He totaled 16,726 yards rushing in his distinguished career. He retired in 1987 and was diagnosed in 1999 with a rare liver condition that required a transplant. Payton never received a transplant, however, as he developed cancer in the affected area. He died shortly thereafter.

The inexhaustible Walter Payton broke Jim Brown's all-time National Football League (NFL) rushing mark in 1984. His gridiron feats prompted one reporter to question the two-time Most Valuable Player (MVP) about his uncanny talent.

"How would you try to stop Walter Payton if you were on the other team?" the reporter asked. The running back answered, "Well, the night before the game, I'd kidnap Walter Payton."

Walter Jerry Payton was born on July 25, 1954, in Columbia, Mississippi. He grew up among fine football players. Older brother Eddie became a solid NFL performer, as did his uncle, Rickey Young.

Payton bulls his way for more yardage.

Payton, Walter

Payton powers over the Kansas City defense for a touchdown. His amazing leg strength made him difficult to stop near the goal line.

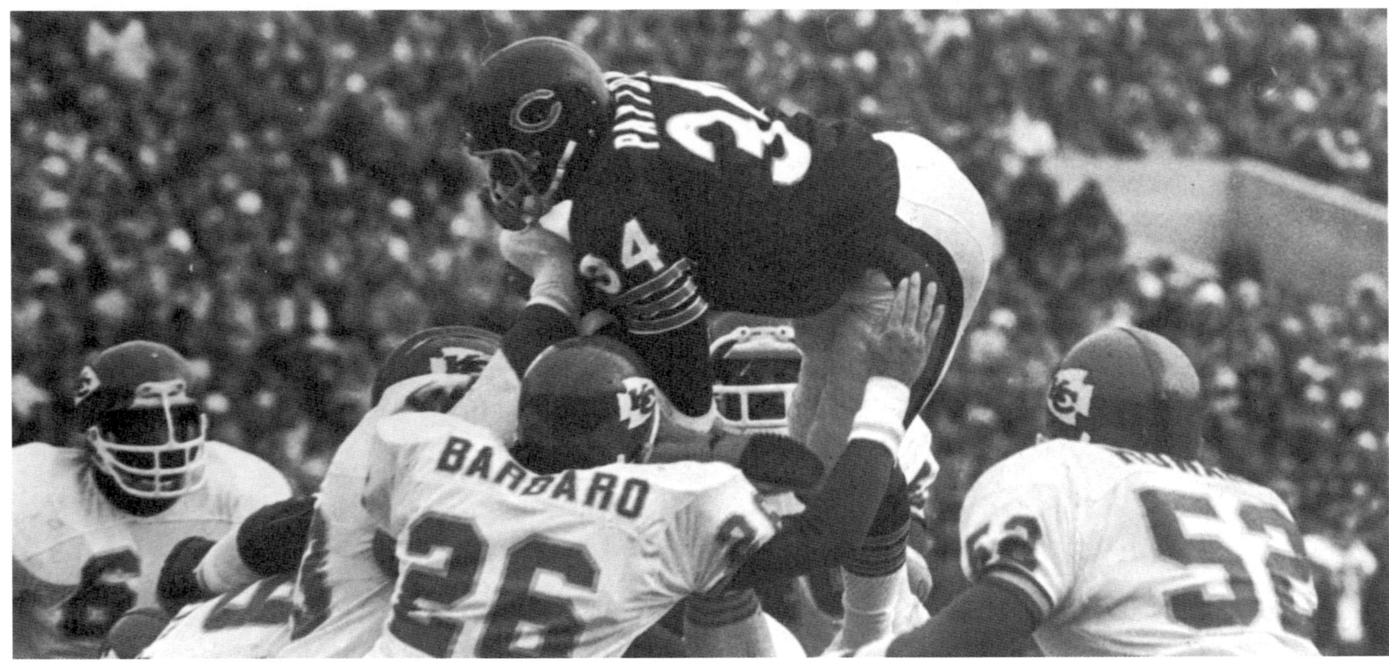

Walter started playing football with the members of his family. Soon, he began to develop as a running back. Building his strength was the key to his later success. "I worked on getting my legs and upper body almost evenly proportioned, strengthwise," he recalled. "I wanted them to be flexible." Payton became an awesome physical specimen, standing 5 feet, 10 inches, and weighing over 200 pounds.

As a collegian, he was easy for pro scouts to spot. At Jackson State University in Mississippi, he rushed for 3563 yards and scored 464 points in four years. In his junior year, he scored 160 points to lead the nation in scoring. But Walter was not only an excellent rusher. He was a fine receiver and kick returner, and the team's punter and placekicker. He was also a good passer, completing 14 of 19 attempts during his college career.

It was Payton's running, however—his combination of bulling over tacklers and darting through opposing lines—that attracted the pro scouts. The Chicago Bears made Walter Payton their first draft choice for the 1975 season. He was the first running back chosen in the draft.

Professional Development

Payton was a good, solid rookie. He gained 679 yards in 196 rushing attempts in 1975. He also established himself as a superb blocker. Near the end of the season, the Bears learned just how good he was. In the final game against the New Orleans Saints, Payton piled up 134 yards rushing and 102 yards on two kickoff returns.

Walter more than doubled his rushing yardage as a second-year pro. With 1390 yards in 1976, he earned the National Football Conference (NFC) rushing title. The league's players were getting to know Walter Payton.

"When God said, 'I'm going to build me the best football players who ever lived,' he made Jim Thorpe and Walter Payton."

—Chicago Bears coach Mike Ditka

Payton goes up and over for a first down.

O. J. Simpson, a star running back during the 1970s, referred to Payton as an "insane runner." Simpson meant it as a compliment and added, "I mean there often is no rhyme or reason to what the runner does, but it all works out. It's an instinct."

Walter relied on more than just instinct. He took pride in his amazing strength. "I get stronger as the game goes on," he said. "In the first quarter, I get a little winded. I'm strongest during the end of the second, when I get started, and during the third and fourth quarters."

Payton could take the pounding the league's defenders had to offer. He was also more than willing to pound his opponents. He stated, "One of my objectives is, if I'm going to get hit, why let the guy who's going to hit me get the easiest and best shot. I'll make it as hard for him as it is for me. I explode into the guy who's trying to tackle me."

Career Highlights

In 1977, Payton enjoyed his best season. He rushed for 100 yards or more in one game after another. In late October, he rushed for 205 yards in 23 carries against the Green Bay Packers.

On November 20, against the powerful defense of the Minnesota Vikings, Walter proved his toughness and durability. Despite a bout with the flu that kept him in bed on Thursday and Friday, Payton was in uniform on Sunday and ready to go to work.

Payton, Walter

In the first quarter, he carried 13 times and gained 77 yards. By halftime, he had 26 carries and 144 yards. Running mostly power plays and sweeps to the right side, he kept coming at the Vikings in the second half. After three quarters, he had carried the ball 34 times for 192 yards.

The NFL rushing mark for most yards gained in one game was 273, held by O. J. Simpson. With five minutes left, Walter needed 63 more yards for the record. His shot at the all-time mark seemed unlikely.

Career Highlights

Scored a college-record 464 points in his collegiate career

Rushed for 275 yards in a single game in 1977

Led Chicago Bears to 1986 Super Bowl victory

Ranks second all-time in rushing yardage

Two-time NFL Most Valuable Player

Rushed for over 16,000 yards—nearly 10 miles—in his career

Payton hurdles over Detroit defenders.

Payton called upon his late-game strength. Plowing over the right tackle, he burst for 58 yards before going out of bounds. He gained three more yards on a sweep. On his 40th and final carry, he gained four yards around right end to give him a record 275. (This record stood until September 14, 2003, when Jamal Lewis of the Baltimore Ravens rushed for 295 yards in a single game against the Cleveland Browns.)

Payton rushed for 1852 yards in 1977. Only Simpson and Jim Brown had ever carried the ball for more yardage in one campaign. After the season ended, Walter was an All-Pro choice, and was named NFL Player of the Year and the United Press International (UPI) Athlete of the Year. Perhaps the greatest praise came from an opposing coach, Monte Clark of the Detroit Lions. "Jimmy Brown was the greatest of all time," he said, "but Payton is as good as any of the others. He scares me to death."

Payton was forever giving credit to his linemen and to his blocking back, Roland Harper. After scoring touchdowns, Walter did not spike the ball in the end zone. Instead, he handed the ball to his teammates for the ceremonial gesture. His teammates, in turn, honored him with over a dozen game balls in his first few seasons. The Chicago Bears front office rewarded Payton generously for his great talent. Walter became the highest-paid player in NFL history.

Payton continued to punish opponents and carry the Chicago Bears on his shoulders. He led the NFC in rushing every year from 1978 through 1980. In 1979, the durable back carried the ball on runs and passes 402 times—an NFL record.

From 1976 through 1980, Payton led the NFC in rushing.

A Football Legend

Walter worked extremely hard to stay in top shape. During off-seasons, he ran "the Hill," a steeply angled pile of dirt, 12 to 15 times a day. He could bench-press 390 pounds and could do a set of leg presses at 700 pounds.

"He's got the strongest legs I've ever seen. They are like springs," exclaimed Washington's general manager, Bobby Beathard. "If he had played on consistently good teams, oh, my gosh, I can't imagine what he would have accomplished."

Payton's strength was near legendary. One year, after dislocating a shoulder in training camp, Walter told Bears trainer Fred Caito that he could play despite the injury. To prove it, he jumped off the training table and walked on his hands down the hallway. Caito was stunned. When healthy, Walter could walk the width of a football field on his hands.

The year 1984 was a special one for Walter Payton. That year, he broke Jim Brown's all-time rushing record of 12,312 yards. He accomplished the feat on a six-yard sweep against the New Orleans Saints. The game was stopped for three minutes while

Payton, Walter

Walter and his brother Eddie (left) leave the field following a 1977 exhibition game. Eddie played defensive back for the Cleveland Browns.

Payton received the game ball.

In 1984, Walter ran for a 72-yard touchdown, the longest of his career. He also set the all-time records for rushing attempts and combined yardage, and he broke Brown's record of 58 100-yard rushing games.

The next year, Payton gained 1551 yards rushing and caught 49 passes for 483 yards, surpassing 2000 combined yards for the third straight season—another NFL record. More important, the Bears reached the Super Bowl, where they crushed the New England Patriots, 46–10. Payton received the 1985 Jim Thorpe Trophy as the league's most valuable player.

Walter's boundless energy served him well off the field. He enjoyed hunting and fishing, and he was an accomplished drummer. "Sweetness," as he was often called, was also a great dancer. He once competed in the national dance finals of the television show *Soul Train*.

Payton always seemed to be doing things for kids—throwing benefits for the sick and lending a helping hand to troubled ones. The Bears' public relations office called Walter when there was something to be done for children.

Entering his twelfth campaign in 1986, Payton had missed only one game in his career. That year, he recorded his tenth 1000-yard rushing season, establishing another league mark. He also became the first player to accumulate 20,000 all-purpose yards. He appeared in his eighth Pro Bowl that season.

By 1987, Payton had scored 100 rushing touchdowns and made 492 receptions. When he retired after the season, Walter held the career marks for yards rushing (16,726), attempts rushing (3838), and combined yards (21,803). His total number of touchdowns (125) was only one shy of Jim Brown's record. Emmitt Smith finally broke Payton's yards rushing record in

"Walter was a Chicago icon long before I arrived there. He was a great man off the field and his on-field accomplishments speak for themselves."

—Michael Jordan

Eluding the lunges of defenders, Payton darts toward the end zone.

2002, fifteen years later. The Bears retired Walter's jersey number, 34, before his final regular-season home game in 1987.

In a true testament to Payton's all-around greatness, Bears head coach Mike Ditka once stated: "When God said, 'I'm going to build me the best football players who ever lived,' he made Jim Thorpe and Walter Payton."

After his retirement, Walter Payton was inducted into the Pro Football Hall of Fame in 1993. In 1999, Payton revealed that he was suffering from a rare liver disease and needed a transplant. Cancer in the bile duct eventually cost Walter Payton his life, but praise for "Sweetness" came from all corners of the football world, both for the football player and the person. Jarrett Payton, Walter's son, wore his father's number 34 as a running back for the University of Miami Hurricanes. And, after scoring his first collegiate touchdown in 2001, he dedicated the score to his late father in a memorable tribute.

Further Study

BOOKS

Gallagher, Aileen. *Walter Payton.* New York, NY: Rosen Central, 2003.

Johnson, Tom and David Fantle. *Sweetness: The Courage and Heart of Walter Peyton.* Chicago, IL: Triumph Books, 1999.

Koslow, Philip. *Walter Peyton.* New York, NY: Chelsea House Publishers, 1994.

WEB SITES

"Walter Payton," *Pro Football Hall of Fame.* Online at www.profootballhof.com/index.cfm?section=team&cont_id=player&personnel_id=1322&roster_id=42 (November 2003)

Pelé

Pelé (1940–), soccer player, was born Edson Arantes do Nascimento in Tres Coracoes, Brazil. At 15, he joined the Santos, Brazil, soccer team. Pelé led Santos to several major state-league titles, including six in a row. He led the Brazilian National Team to World Cup victories in 1958, 1962, and 1970. His greatest years were in the early 1960s, when he teamed up with Coutinho to create one of the greatest scoring combinations of all time. In 1969, he became the first player ever to score 1000 career goals. Pelé retired from the Brazilian National Team in 1971 and the Santos team in October 1974. Eight months later, he signed a multimillion-dollar, three-year contract with the New York Cosmos of the North American Soccer League (NASL). He was largely responsible for the soccer boom in the United States. Pelé led the Cosmos to the 1977 NASL championship.

On October 1, 1977, the Santos Club of Brazil played an exhibition game against the New York Cosmos. But this was no simple practice game. Over 76,000 fans braved a pouring rain to pack Giants Stadium in New Jersey. They had come to say goodbye to Pelé, the most brilliant soccer player in history. The "Black Pearl" had announced earlier that this would be his last game.

Pelé played the first half with the Cosmos. During his three years with New York, he had helped popularize soccer in the United States. At halftime, Pelé switched jerseys and played the rest of the game with Santos, the team on which he had starred for the first 19 years of his career. Even at 37, the Great One dazzled the crowd with his grace, speed, and uncanny ball control abilities. At the end of the game, the fans stood for a final farewell, chanting, "Pelé! Pelé!"

The feats of Brazil's greatest athlete are known to more people in the world than those of any athlete before him. Pelé's career began quietly in the village of Três Coraçoes in the state of Minas Gerais, Brazil. He was named Edson Arantes do Nascimento when he was born on October 23, 1940. As a young soccer player he soon earned the nickname "Pelé"—a name that became known throughout much of the world. His father, João Ramos do Nascimento—called Dondinho—was also a soccer player. Pelé began playing soccer with a

Pelé makes use of his head to bounce a pass to a teammate.

rag-filled makeshift ball. When he was 10, he quit school and began to concentrate on developing his natural talents.

A retired player from the São Paulo team, Waldemar de Brito, recognized Pelé's potential when he saw him in a pickup game when the boy was 11. For four years, the older player worked with young Pelé until he felt he was ready for a big team. De Brito felt that the 15-year-old would be "the greatest player in the world." But the big São Paulo teams did not want the youngster, so de Brito took Pelé to his own former team in Santos, São Paulo's port city. There, in 1956, in his first professional soccer game, young Pelé scored four goals, leading Santos to a 7–1 victory.

In soccer, called "football" in the world outside the United States, the scoring is normally quite low. A soccer goal has been compared to a home run in baseball. Four home runs in a rookie player's first big league ball game would alert the fans that a great new star was on his way. So it was with Pelé's four-goal achievement in his first game. He was on his way.

Life As A Pro

By the time Pelé was 16, in his second year as a pro, he had earned a secure place on the Santos first team. Within a year, he had been named to the national team and played in a game against Argentina.

Already a veteran at 17, Pelé was selected for Brazil's 1958 World Cup team. An injury kept him from play until the quarterfinal round against Wales. Then, with one of the most important goals of his career, Pelé scored the game's only point. Brazil moved into the semifinals. Pelé scored three more goals in the semifinal game against France and two in the final game against Sweden. His superstar performance brought Pelé worldwide attention and Brazil's undying gratitude. It was the first World Cup championship for Brazil and

Pelé

Pelé in one of his most memorable moments—scoring his 1000th goal, then donning a special jersey for the occasion.

the beginning of Brazilian dominance of world football.

Although Pelé's scoring feats were record-shattering—he scored 125 goals in 1958 alone—that skill was not his only strength. He developed a cunning that enabled him to lope downfield with the ball, waiting for the split second in which to accelerate, catching the defense off guard. As if the ball were tied to his foot, Pelé could explode from a standstill, race with the ball, and stop just as suddenly—all with full control of the ball.

No player in the history of the game has equaled his ability to deaden any ball from flight and assume control of it, even at full speed. The 5-foot, 8-inch, 160-pounder could leap above taller defenders to "head" home goals. He even used the legs of his opponents to his own advantage, by rebounding passes off them and back to himself as he skillfully maneuvered past the baffled opposition.

Pelé's greatest years with Santos were during the early

At a special ceremony in 1969, Pelé cancels the first of two million stamps issued by Brazil to honor his 1000th goal. A reproduction of the stamp is in the upper right hand corner.

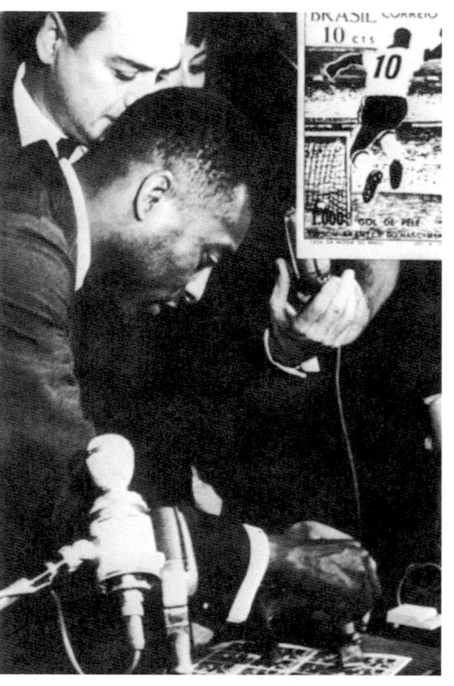

1960s. Teamed with Coutinho, he was part of one of the most awesome striker combinations of all time. The "King of Soccer" scored 1220 goals during his career from 1956 to 1974. It was his 1000th point that drew what was probably the widest news coverage in the history of sports. On November 19, 1969, in the national stadium in Rio de Janeiro, Pelé hit the 1000-point mark. One hundred thousand fans shrieked in joy as they watched the nimble athlete make his unprecedented score.

Pelé played for Brazil's World Cup team again in Chile in 1962, but was sidelined by an

"'How do you spell Pelè?' G-O-D."
—The Sunday Times, *British newspaper*

Sports stars are always popular figures among autograph seekers, and Pelé is no exception.

injury in the second game against Czechoslovakia. (In 1993, Czechoslovaki broke into two separate countries—Czech Republic and Slovakia.) He had to sit out the rest of the series. Brazil won the competition, even without his participation. Again in the 1966 World Cup, held this time in England, Pelé was on the team. He scored in the opening game, but he was injured in the second match against Hungary. Pelé returned to play against Portugal, but he was brutally tackled and injured again. Pelé announced that he would never play in another World Cup event.

But Brazil had not won the 1966 match, and by 1970 they were eager to be the first team to win three World Cup competitions. Brazil would retire the Jules Rimet Trophy if they had a third win.

When the 1970 World Cup opened in Mexico City, Pelé was there. He scored six times in six games to help Brazil qualify. Then he scored four more times, including a brilliant head goal that gave Brazil the lead in the final game against Italy. Brazil won by a score of 4–1. They became the first

Career Highlights

Scored four goals in his first professional game

Led Santos to six consecutive state-league championships

Helped Brazil win three World Cups (1958, 1962, 1970)

First player to score over 1000 career goals

Won 1977 NASL Championship with the New York Cosmos

Named Athlete of the Century in 1999 by the International Olympic Committee

Pelé

With a burst of speed, Pelé streaks by an opponent to pick up a loose ball.

three-time winner in World Cup competition.

Shortly after the game, Pelé announced that he would not play in the next World Cup matches in 1974. The Great One was retiring from international competition.

His last game with the Brazilian Nationals was on July 18, 1971, against Yugoslavia. (By the early 1990s, Yugoslavia had broken up into five separate countries.) He played the first half of the game, and then trotted around the track as the 130,000 fans that packed the stadium gave him an emotional farewell.

Pelé continued to play with the Santos team, leading them to the 1973 São Paulo state championship for the 11th time in 14 years. He also played exhibition games throughout the world. By then one of the richest men in Brazil, he decided to retire and devote his time to his family and his many business interests. Pelé's last game with Santos was in October 1974.

Coming to America

But he did not stay retired long. The New York Cosmos of the North American Soccer League (NASL) offered him an estimated $4.7 million to play three seasons in the United States. Pelé saw it as a chance to promote soccer in a country where it was not a big sport. In June 1975, he joined the Cosmos.

Great excitement accompanied Pelé's appearances, as American sports fans paid tribute to the world's richest and most famous athlete. Playing in the NASL, Pelé gave worldwide credibility to the league. Other great international soccer stars followed him to North America, including George Best and Franz Beckenbauer.

The league's Most Valuable Player in 1976, Pelé played through the 1977 season with the Cosmos. That year, New York captured the NASL championship, climaxing Pelé's three years in the league. For the title, the Cosmos defeated the Seattle Sounders, 2–1.

After the victory, the "Black Pearl" remarked, "Now I know I have accomplished what I came

With the Arc de Triomphe in Paris in the background, Pelé rides down the Champs Elysees amid a crowd of cheering Frenchmen. The trophy in his hand is symbolic of Brazil's World Cup victory in 1970.

"It's fantastic, all over the world people respect and love me. It's unbelievable if you think I stopped playing more than 25 years ago."

—Pelé on his worldwide popularity

President Bill Clinton gets a soccer lesson from Pelé during an event in Brazil.

here for—to make soccer a reality in the U.S." Pelé finished his fantastic career with 1282 career goals to his name.

After his retirement, Pelé published several best-selling biographies and starred in a number of documentary films including *Pelé* in 1977. He also composed the soundtrack for the film. In 1999, the International Olympic Committee name Pelé the Athlete of the Century, a fitting honor for a man who contributed so much to his sport.

Further Study

BOOKS

Arnold, Caroline. *Pelé: King of Soccer.* New York, NY: F. Watts, 1992.

Harris, Harry. *Pelé: His Life and Times.* New York, NY: Welcome Rain Publishers, 2002.

Herzog, Brad. *The 20 Greatest Athletes of the 20th Century.* New York, NY: Rosen Publishing Group, 2003.

WEB SITES

"Pelé," *International Football Hall of Fame.* Online at www.ifhof.com/hof/Pelé.asp (November 2003)

Peppler, Mary Jo

Mary Jo Peppler (1944–), volleyball player, was born in Rockford, Illinois. After moving to California, Mary Jo Peppler played on volleyball teams around the Los Angeles area and developed into an excellent player as a teenager. She was a member of the 1964 U.S. Olympic team while attending Los Angeles State University. Later, she helped form the Los Angeles Renegades volleyball team. In 1965, Mary Jo led them to the amateur national championship. In 1967, she led the American team to victory in the Pan American Games. Working for a master's degree at Sul Ross State University in Alpine, Texas, Peppler organized a volleyball team that won two national collegiate championships. In 1970, Mary Jo was voted the best player in the World Volleyball Championship Games in Bourgas, Bulgaria. As player-coach, she led the E Pluribus Unum team from Houston, Texas, to national championships in 1972 and 1973. Turning professional in 1974, Mary Jo won the television-staged women's Superstars competition and found success as a player-coach with the New York Liberties in Major League Volleyball. She was inducted into the Volleyball Hall of Fame in 1990.

Volleyball great Mary Jo Peppler once said, "When I execute properly, I get a great satisfaction that's independent even of winning or losing. I guess this stems from all those years in volleyball when I was trying to win an Olympic gold medal. Perfection became a goal."

She never did win an Olympic gold medal or get national recognition in her best years. But in the late 1960s and early 1970s, Mary Jo was one of the top women athletes in the world. Ironically, it was not in volleyball that she was finally noticed. In 1974, she proved her talent in the televised women's Superstars competition, which pitted top athletes against each other in a number of events. Mary Jo Peppler beat many well-established stars to waltz home with a victory.

Mary Jo Peppler was born in Rockford, Illinois, on October 17, 1944. Her family lived in

Playing for the Phoenix Heat, Peppler sets up a teammate during a 1976 contest.

several places around the country when she was young. Most of her teenage years were spent in California. She was always athletically talented, and wherever she lived, Mary Jo was involved in sports.

In southern California, volleyball is more popular than in other parts of the country. There, Mary Jo began playing the game as part of her social life.

"If I had been smart, I would have gone into a sport like tennis," she later reflected. "Volleyball was more a group sport with us. All the guys and girls would pile into an old car and go to the park and play volleyball together."

By 1962, her senior year in high school, Mary Jo was good enough to play with the women's national championship volleyball team, the Long Beach Shamrocks. She left them to join the Los Angeles Spartans, a team on which she would get more playing time. She helped lead the Spartans to a runner-up spot in the national competition.

Getting Serious about Volleyball

Mary Jo was developing into one of the best volleyball players in the country. While attending Los Angeles State University, she made the 1964 Olympic team. Even though volleyball originated in the United States, the American team was no match for most of the teams from the other countries. At the Olympics in Tokyo, Japan, the U.S. women's volleyball squad finished fifth among six teams.

Back in Los Angeles, Mary Jo helped form the Los Angeles Renegades. The team staffed the 6-foot Peppler on the front line. In 1965, the Renegades won the amateur national championship.

In 1967, Peppler led the American volleyball team to victory at the Pan American Games. The best player in the United States, Mary Jo looked forward to winning a medal in the 1968 Olympics. But neither the coach nor the other players on the Olympic team were in her class. Realizing that it would be a rerun of 1964, Mary Jo quit the team.

"The coach had no game plans or strategy," she later said, "and I saw no reason to be humiliated in international competition while the whole world was watching."

Shortly afterward, Mary Jo moved to Texas to finish a master's degree at Sul Ross State University

Peppler, Mary Jo

Peppler leaps high for a spike during a practice session with the El Paso-Juarez Sol.

in Alpine. With a friend, Marilyn McReavy, she built a volleyball team at Sul Ross that won two national collegiate titles.

In 1970, Mary Jo and four teammates joined the U.S. team for the World Volleyball Championship Games in Bourgas, Bulgaria. Even though the team placed a poor 11th, Mary Jo Peppier was voted the best player in the tournament. Her coach, Val Keller, described her as "the best woman volleyball player in the world, bar none."

For the same reasons she had quit the 1968 Olympic team, Mary Jo boycotted the 1972 U.S. effort. She and Marilyn McReavy became player-coaches of the E Pluribus Unum team in Houston, Texas. Possibly the best amateur team ever, it won back-to-back national championships in 1972 and 1973.

In 1974, Mary Jo had big hopes of winning a gold medal using players from her Texas team as a nucleus for the 1976 Olympic squad. But the new coach of the American team did not appreciate Mary Jo's talent or her strong-willed personality.

"Women's athletics is wide open now. It's an exciting time to be in the field."
—Mary Jo Peppler

Once again, she quit the team in disgust. She decided to move on to the professional level.

"It's self-defeating to be a amateur athlete today," she said bitterly, "and that's basically what most women athletes are—amateurs."

Life As a Pro

During her many years as a amateur, Mary Jo had struggled to support herself with a variety of jobs. One of her first money-making athletic ventures was the 1974 women's Superstars competition promoted by American Broadcasting Company (ABC) television. Virtually unknown to the general public, she was chosen for the event as a last-minute substitute when one of the more famous athletes dropped out.

Winning four events and $15,500 in the preliminaries, she earned a place in the finals at Rotunda, Florida. There, Mary Jo placed first in the softball throw, in basketball shooting, and in the rowing competition.

Doing well in some of the other events, she narrowly defeated basketball star Karen Logan for the overall victory. Mary Jo earned $34,100 (equal to more than $125,000 in 2003) for her winning efforts.

In 1975, Peppler became one of the stars on the El Paso-Juarez Sol professional team. The squad was part of the new International Volleyball Association (IVA), in which men and women played together.

The next year, she was player-coach of the Phoenix Heat in the IVA. An inventive leader, she was named the league's coach of the year.

"It was an honor because it recognized me as a woman coach," Peppler told Evelyn Lawrence, who featured her in a story in *Sportswoman* magazine. "I've never been too impressed by awards, though. My pleasure comes in being a success as a coach—I love it."

At 42, Mary Jo Peppler became player-coach of the New York Liberties in 1987. The team was part of Major League Volleyball, the first professional league for U.S. women.

For years she struggled to reach perfection. But as a woman in a minor sport, she had not gained the money or recognition many great athletes take for granted. She looked forward to contributing to the growth of women's intercollegiate sports programs.

"Women's athletics is wide open now," said coach Peppler. "It's an exciting time to be in the field."

Further Study

Peppler, Mary Jo. *Inside Volleyball for Women*. Chicago, IL: H. Regnery, 1977.

Career Highlights

A member of the Volleyball Hall of Fame since 1990

Six-time First-Team All American and four-time Player of the Year, winning her first award in 1967 and her last in 1981

Five-time member of the USA Women's National team, winning a silver medal at the 1984 Olympics in Los Angeles and a gold medal at the Pan Am Games in 1967

Four-time member of a Women's Open National Championship team.

In 1984, was selected as a USVBA All-Time Great Female Player.

Petty, Richard

Richard Petty (1937–), race driver, was born in Level Cross, North Carolina. His father was a successful stock car driver and Richard was anxious to follow suit. He began racing in 1958 and was named Rookie of the Year on the National Association for Stock Car Auto Racing (NASCAR) Grand National circuit. In 1960, Petty won his first race. In 1984, he won his 200th NASCAR event. He captured his first national driving championship in 1964. He won it again in 1967, 1971, 1972, 1974, 1975, and 1979. In 1967, Petty set a record no one will ever approach. He won 27 of 48 races—10 of those victories in a row. His seven wins in the Daytona 500 are unmatched. "The King" earned over $7.5 million during his illustrious 35-year career. The all-time-winningest driver in NASCAR history, Richard Petty became the first to claim both his father (Lee) and his son (Kyle) as winners of NASCAR races.

Few people have dominated a sport as Richard Petty has. In the world of stock car racing, Petty was the best. His fans called him "The King."

Petty was voted stock car racing's most popular driver nine times. He started 1185 races and won 200—nearly twice as many victories as anyone else. His 55 super speedway victories included seven Daytona 500 wins. He finished in the top five 555 times and in the top ten 712 times. All of those marks set records for the National Association for Stock Car Auto Racing (NASCAR).

In addition, Richard Petty captured the national driving title (also known as the Winston Cup championship) seven times (1964, 1967, 1971, 1972, 1974, 1975, and 1979). Only Dale Earnhardt won as many Winston Cup championships.

In the stock car world, praise from one driver for another is seldom heard. The men are highly competitive and give nothing away. "Other drivers may be better on a given day, but it seems like Richard is there every day," said rival David Pearson. "He drives smart and hard, and he has to be one of the best ever. And you have to respect his record, which is the best ever."

Petty takes a brief rest from his racing activities to pose with his car.

The Early Years

Richard Petty was born in Level Cross, North Carolina, on July 2, 1937. His father, Lee, was a garage mechanic who ran cars for fun on the back roads around town. When Richard was 10, Lee drove his first NASCAR race and quickly became one of the best.

Richard was an all-around athlete who played football, baseball, and basketball in high school. From age 12, he helped his father work on stock cars. It was only natural for him to begin racing.

"My daddy was a race driver, so I became a race driver," Richard once said. "If he'd been a grocer, I might have been a grocer."

There were two races available one weekend in 1958, and Lee could not run in both. So Richard asked if he might try one. Lee had no objections to the idea, and Richard began his incredible career.

The Rookie Years

Richard entered nine races that year and finished in the top ten in one of them. His ability got a lot of attention and he was voted the 1958 NASCAR Rookie of the Year.

The first couple of seasons were hard for the young man. He

"He drives smart and hard, and he has to be one of the best ever. And you have to respect his record, which is the best ever."

—David Pearson, driver

Petty, Richard

Petty goes to the pits for fuel and tires during the Daytona 500.

tore up a lot of his father's racing equipment and brought home little money. But the older Petty helped with the finances and taught his son the ways of the track. They raced against each other for four years before an accident in 1961 ended Lee's career as a driver.

In 1960, Richard Petty entered 40 races and won three of them. He placed second in point standings for the driving championship. Stock car racing had a new star.

He placed second again in 1962 and 1963. He won 14 races in the latter year. He was entering 40 to 50 races a year, and his wins were coming on the shorter tracks.

His first super-speedway win came in 1964 at the Daytona 500. Petty dominated the last 350 miles and set a record average speed of more than 154 miles per hour. He won eight other races that year, finishing in the top five 37 times. Richard Petty also captured the first of his seven driving titles.

Of all the tracks Petty drove in his brilliant career, he found the Daytona International Speedway in Daytona Beach, Florida, best fitted to his driving skills. He won the Daytona 500 seven times—more than any other driver.

Petty said that he was just keeping the event in the family, since his father won the first Daytona 500 in 1959. Petty made those long grinds look easy. He won 500-mile races a record 41 times.

Driver + Team = Wins

Petty's best year was 1967, when he set the single-season victory record with an incredible 27. He also established another mark by scoring 10 wins in a row. It was the beginning of a great five years. He won 16 races in 1968, 10 in 1969, 18 in 1970, and 21 in 1971.

Petty gave much of the credit for his success to his crew, winners of the 1976 pit stop championships: "I don't depend just on Richard Petty; I depend on Petty Enterprises. My daddy runs the team—not as much as he used to maybe, but when he's there he's the boss. My engine builder is my brother Maurice, and my crew chief is my cousin Dale Inman. I'm a team man, and in the long run a team man will win more than an individualist."

But Richard was a great driver. He liked to take the lead from the start and let the other drivers blow their engines trying to catch him. He was not as strong as some drivers, but Petty was a thinker.

Petty, with his trademark cowboy hat and sunglasses, takes a minute to relax next to his car before a NASCAR qualifying race in 1981.

Smooth and consistent, Richard had the touch. Although there were fewer races on the circuit in the 1970s, he kept winning—10 in 1974 and 13 in 1975.

The first driver to have a national fan club, Petty spent hour after hour signing autographs, rarely turning down a request. He dedicated the 1992 season, his 35th as a NASCAR driver, to his fans. It was his last year as a driver. After his retirement, Petty was awarded several honors, including receiving the Medal of Freedom in 1992 and induction to the International Motor Sports Hall of Fame in 1997.

The Petty winning tradition would continue in the years ahead. Richard's son, Kyle, emerged as one of the hottest NASCAR Winston Cup drivers in 1992. And Richard stayed active as a car owner in Winston Cup racing.

Five-time NASCAR champion, the late Dale Earnhardt remarked, "Richard Petty has always given back to racing more than he's taken out, and that's a record that will probably always stand."

Further Study

BOOKS

Bongard, Tim and Bill Coulter. *The Cars of the King*. Champaign, IL: Sports Publishing, 1997.

Frankl, Ron. *Richard Petty*. New York, NY: Chelsea House Publishers, 1996.

Teitelbaum, Michael. *Richard Petty, "The King"*. Excelsior, MN: Tradition Publishing, 2002.

WEB SITES

Petty Racing. Online at www.pettyracing.com (November 2003)

Career Highlights

Seven-time winner of Daytona 500

Seven-time NASCAR national champ (1964, 1967, 1971, 1972, 1974, 1975, 1979)

Became first stock car driver to win $1 million in a career

All-time NASCAR leader in races won (200)

Won 27 races, including 10 straight, in 1967

Phelps, Michael

Michael Phelps (1985–), swimmer, was born June 30, 1985 in Baltimore, Maryland. In 2000, Phelps became the youngest male to compete in the Olympic Games since 1932. At age 15, he finished fifth in the 200-meter butterfly. In the spring of 2001, he became the youngest man to break a swimming world record by posting a time of 1:54.97 in the 200-meter butterfly. At the 2002 Summer Nationals, Phelps shattered the American record in the 200-meter individual medley with the third-fastest time in history.

He became the first man to win five U.S. National titles at one championship. Later in the year, Phelps captured six gold medals and broke five world records at the World Championships. The 18-year-old surpassed legendary Mark Spitz for most world records set in individual events at a single swim meet.

It was football season in Baltimore. The Ravens were in the 2003 NFL playoffs. Football fans packed the stadium eagerly awaiting the opening kickoff. The officials called the captains to the 50-yard line for the coin toss. Pro-Bowl quarterback Steve McNair represented the Titans. For the Ravens, out walked superstar linebacker Ray Lewis and—as an honorary captain—a teenage swimmer named Michael Phelps. It was a great honor for a great young swimmer.

Michael Phelps was born June 30, 1985 to parents Fred and Debbie Phelps. His mother was a schoolteacher until she became an administrator for the Baltimore schools. His father is a Maryland state trooper.

A natural athlete, he played lacrosse, soccer, and baseball, but excelled at swimming. It was no surprise. His two older sisters were terrific swimmers. Hilary was a national-class competitor and Whitney was a member of the 1994 World Championship team.

Following in his sisters' footsteps, Michael began swimming at age 6. Like many little kids, Michael didn't like getting his face wet. But with a little practice he learned to love the water. At age 7, he joined the North Baltimore Aquatic Club (NBAC), a prestigious swimming team near his home. NBAC swimmers have won five Olympic gold medals and set 15 world records. There he met coach Bob Bowman. Bowman

Michael Phelps clocks a new world record with a time of 1:57.52 during the men's 200-meter individual medley at the 2003 FINA World Swimming Championships.

PHELPS

Phelps, Michael

Swimming
Words to Know

dolphin kick
A kick that is performed by holding the legs together and moving them up and down while bending at the knee. It is used in the butterfly stroke and sometimes by backstrokers at starts and turns.

gravity wave
Turbulence caused by the motion of a swimmer moving through the water. The swimmer's body pushes the water forward and down towards the bottom of the pool. This action creates a wave that bounces off the bottom of the pool and returns to the surface as turbulence.

individual medley (IM)
The event in which the swimmer swims the first quarter of the distance using the butterfly, the next quarter using the backstroke, the next quarter using the breaststroke, and the final quarter using the freestyle.

split time
A time recorded at the end of every 50 meters in a race. It is used to gauge the swimmer's pace. A negative split occurs when a swimmer swims faster in the second half of the race than in the first in order to gain a strategic advantage.

surf
The wave created by a lead swimmer. Swimmers in adjacent lanes may swim just behind the leader in an attempt to take advantage of the wave.

would help him blossom into one of the sport's biggest stars.

Bowman was used to working with good swimmers and Phelps was the best he had ever seen. One day Coach Bowman took Phelps aside and told him something that would change his life. Bowman told Phelps "If you want to focus on something, you could be in the Olympics."

This got Phelps's attention. "When I heard that," Phelps recalled to the *Philadelphia Inquirer*, "I perked my ears up. Everyone, I think, as a little kid wants to do something big, like be in the Olympics. Everyone wants to be the best—an American icon."

Phelps took his coach's advice. He cut back on lacrosse, soccer, and baseball and began to concentrate solely on swimming.

Tall and thin, he had the perfect build for a swimmer. He practiced hard and soon became one of the best young swimmers in the Baltimore area. The NBAC was the place to be if Phelps wanted to reach his potential.

Record-Setting Teenager

Phelps began to dominate the competition. In 2000, although only 15 years old, he qualified for the 2000 Summer Olympics in Sydney, Australia. He was the youngest male Olympian in nearly 70 years. Phelps placed fifth in the 200-meter butterfly. Although he did not earn a medal, Michael Phelps broke the national record in the 15–16 year old age group. The performance was just the beginning of an amazing run to the top of the swimming world.

Phelps, center, smiles for the photographer after receiving one of his gold medals at the 2003 World Championships in Barcelona, Spain.

The following year, at only 16 years old, Michael Phelps made history again. He became the youngest man to break a world record in amateur swimming competition. His time of 1:54.97 in the 200-meter butterfly shattered the world record. Suddenly his name appeared in the record books alongside swimming legends Mark

"Your mind takes you as far as you want to go. It only limits you if you think there is a limit. If you think you can go faster, you can."
—Michael Phelps

Phelps looks towards the stands while toweling off at the 2003 World Championships.

Spitz and Matt Biondi. He beat his own record later in 2001, posting a time of 1:54.58 at the World Championships. USA Swimming named him 2001 Swimmer of the Year. He had conquered the butterfly. Now he went after the other swimming records.

Phelps quickly established himself as one of the best overall swimmers in the world. At the 2002 Summer Nationals, 17-year old Phelps shattered American records in the 200-meter individual medley and the 100-meter butterfly. He also posted a world record mark in the 400-meter individual medley. He added a U.S. Open record in his best event, the 200-meter butterfly.

By now people in the swimming world were starting to compare Phelps to one of the greatest swimmers of all time. "Michael is the closest to Mark Spitz that we have in this country..." said Jon Urbanchek, four-time U.S. Olympic team coach. It was up to Phelps to realize his potential.

A Year to Remember

Michael Phelps's feats in 2003 elevated him to superstar status. He began the year by becoming the first man ever to win a U.S. National title in three different strokes in the same competition. He captured a total of five U.S. National titles. He won the 200-meter individual medley in world record time. He won the 200-meter freestyle and the 400-meter freestyle in American record time. He also won the 200-meter backstroke and the 100-meter freestyle.

Phelps's performance at the 2003 World Championships was even more spectacular. He was named Swimmer of the Meet after collecting six medals, including four golds. He was the first swimmer ever to break five world records in one meet. He broke two world records on the same day. The show left swimming enthusiasts in awe. What he did seemed impossible. Phelps disagreed.

"I wouldn't say anything is impossible. I think that everything is possible as long as you put your mind to it and put the work and time into it," he explained.

Going for the Gold

In May 2003, Phelps graduated from Towson High School. He originally planned to enroll at Loyola College. But that was before

Phelps competes in the backstroke during the 100-meter individual medley at the 2003 World Cup in Melbourne, Australia.

Phelps, Michael

his record-setting performance in the 2003 World Championships. He was now considered one of the best swimmers in the world. College would have to wait. The 2004 Summer Olympic Games in Athens, Greece, were only a year away. Phelps decided to put all of his energy into going for the gold.

Some predicted Phelps could win as many as seven gold medals. When interviewed by Pete Davis of the Loyola College student newspaper, Phelps said "It's hands down the only thing I want...I want an Olympic medal. I don't care if I don't break a world record, I want an Olympic gold medal and right now I'm doing everything I can to at least get one."

Can he match the legendary Mark Spitz? "Mark Spitz is an icon in swimming," said Phelps. "When someone asks you about swimming they say Mark Spitz. That's the only name that pops up in the Olympics—seven gold medals, seven world records. It's in my mind. I think it's in a lot of people's minds, but no one knows who can really truly achieve that. I'm taking one step at a time and if I reach that goal then okay, but that's not the top priority of mine. My top priority is to win an Olympic gold medal."

In 2004, Phelps continued to shine at the Spring Nationals in Orlando, Florida. He claimed five individual titles. Although only 18 years old, he now held 20 national titles, more than any other male swimmer in the past 28 years. But he didn't drop time in the 200-meter individual medley. He went 1:56.80—less than a second off his world record.

When asked by *Baltimore Sun* reporter Paul McMullen about not setting a record, Phelps replied, "As much as you want to, you can't set a world record every race. I'm going home, and getting down and dirty [in practice]. What I had last summer was a lot of endurance. It won't take long to get that back before the [Olympic] trials. Hopefully, that will lead to bigger things."

Career Highlights

In 2000 became the youngest male to compete in the Olympic games since 1932. He finished fifth in the 200m butterfly at age 15.

At the 2001 Spring Nationals he became the youngest man ever to break a world record. He was 15 years, 9 months old when he set the world record in the 200m butterfly

First swimmer to set five world records at one meet at the 2003 World Championships; winning four gold medals and two silver

Only man to ever win a U.S. National title in three different strokes at one national championship

What Does It Take to Be an Olympian?

Michael Phelps is a swimming machine. He is 6-feet, 4-inches tall and weights 195 pounds. He has a large chest and long arms—so long that his wingspan is two inches longer than his body. He has size 14 feet and is especially flexible in the ankles. He has the perfect swimmer's body.

Phelps also pushes his body to the limit. He trains seven day a week.

On weekdays he is up at 6:15 a.m. and in the pool by 7:30. He swims until 9:45, covering over five miles. When he climbs out of the pool he heads to the mats for 15 minutes of what swimmers call dry-land practice. After morning practice, Phelps heads to a local diner for breakfast and then home for a three-hour nap. By 3:45 p.m.

he is back in the water for three more hours of grueling punishment.

"He's a million times more disciplined [than most swimmers]," said fellow Olympic hopeful Jamie Barone. "Almost every day, he's the first one at practice. His tenacity in the pool is crazy. He does things at practice no one has ever done."

Topping off the perfect swimmer's body and incredible work ethic is an overpowering competitive spirit. Above all, Michael Phelps wants to win.

A Bright Future

Phelps earned an endorsement deal with swimwear manufacturer Speedo following his breakout performance of 2003. The endorsement will help pay for Phelps's college education. It will also award him a $1 million bonus if he captures seven gold medals at the 2004 Olympic Games in Athens, Greece. Other national sponsors followed, pushing the total dollar value of Phelps's endorsement contracts to over $6 million.

The future looks bright for Michael Phelps. He has the potential to become the most decorated U.S. swimmer in history. When asked by *The World Today* about his goals, Michael responded, "Is there anything I can't do in the pool? I don't know...I work hard to accomplish my goals, and I do everything I can to accomplish them...the harder you work, the more things you accomplish."

Phelps's swimming gets our attention, but his attitude alone makes him a champion.

Further Study

Coffe, Wayne. "Stroke of Genius." The New York Daily News: January 11, 2004.

Davis, Pete. "Michael Phelps May Bring Global Spotlight to LC." *The Greyhound:* February 17, 2004.

McMullen, Paul. "Phelps' Title Haul at 20 after 200 IM Win." *The Baltimore Sun:* February 15, 2004.

Plante, Jacques

Jacques Plante (1929–1986), hockey player, was born in Mont-Carmel, Quebec, Canada. He joined the Montreal Royals of the Quebec Senior League in 1951 and was called up by the Montreal Canadiens of the National Hockey League (NHL) at the end of 1953. In the next 10 years with Montreal, Plante was an All-Star six times as the Canadiens won five consecutive Stanley Cup championships. He earned the Vezina Trophy six times with the best goals-against average in the league. In 1962 he became the fourth goalie in history to receive the Hart Trophy as the NHL's most valuable player. He won the Vezina Trophy for the seventh time as a member of the St. Louis Blues in 1968. He finished out his illustrious career with the Toronto Maple Leafs, the Boston Bruins, and the Edmonton Oilers. In 838 NHL games, Plante recorded an amazing 82 shutouts and a 2.38 goals-against average. He was even better in the Stanley Cup playoffs, compiling a 2.17 goals-against average and 15 shutouts. A great innovator, Jacques Plante introduced the first plastic goalie mask. In 1978, he was inducted into the Hockey Hall of Fame in his first year of eligibility.

Perhaps, in time, there will come along a National Hockey League (NHL) goaltender who will equal or even surpass Jacques Plante's record of longevity, endurance, and overall brilliance. But that may take a long time. For in 18 NHL seasons, beginning in 1953, the amazing goalie maintained an unmatched quality of excellence. Even at the age of 44, "Jake the Snake"—as Plante was often called—filled in on a team contending for the Stanley Cup, and was a strong factor in helping the Boston Bruins reach the playoffs at the end of the 1972–73 season.

With the Maple Leafs in 1970–71, Plante led the NHL with a 1.88 goals-against average.

1

Plante, Jacques

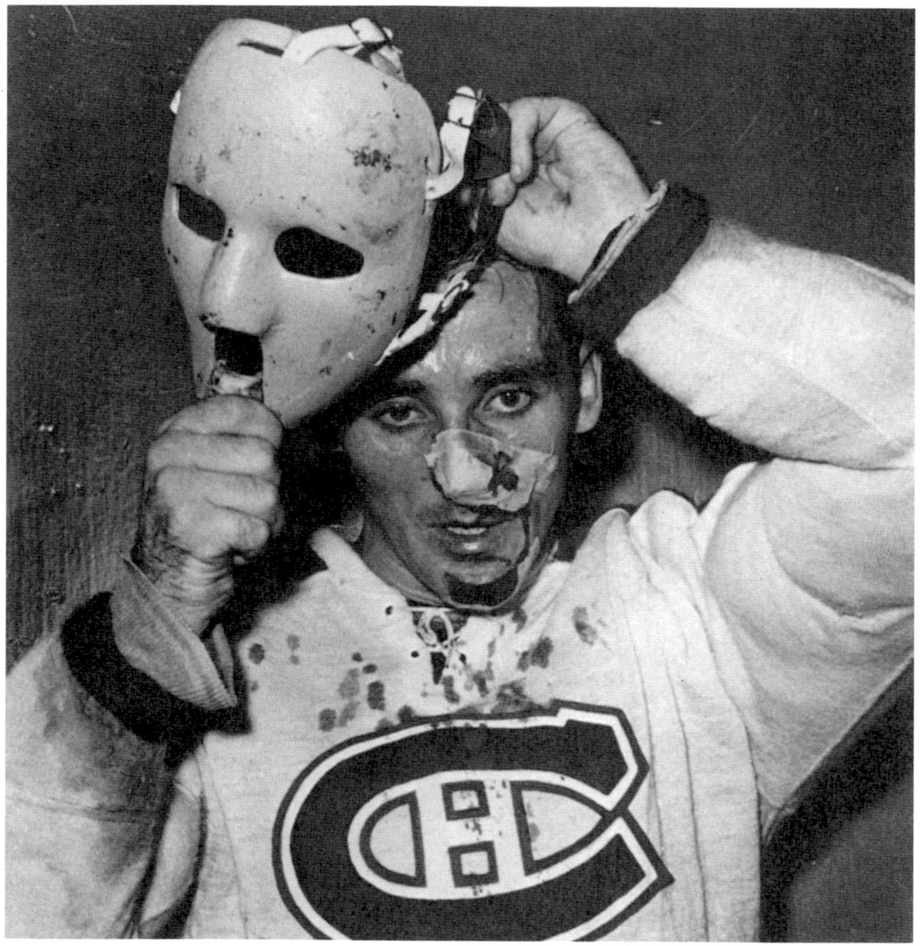

Jacques Plante was the first goaltender in the NHL to wear a mask. After suffering the facial injury shown here, Plante donned the mask he had designed himself. This was the first time he wore the mask in a game.

Joseph Jacques Omar Plante was born January 17, 1929, in Mont-Carmel, Quebec, Canada. He began his hockey career at 15, playing goalie for a factory team in Quebec. At his father's urging, he convinced the coach to pay him 50 cents per game. "Even something as little as 50 cents meant something in those days," Plante recalled later. "We couldn't afford any luxuries at home—not even a radio." Who would have guessed that by 1973 Plante would be signing a million-dollar contract?

It did not take the young Canadian long to start his climb up to hockey's big leagues. Still in his teens, Plante joined the Quebec City team in the junior amateur league for a much-improved salary of $85 a week. From there he advanced to the professional Montreal Royals in the old Quebec Senior League. By the time he was 23, the Montreal Canadiens had heard enough about this promising young player to add him to their squad.

Professional Debut

In his NHL debut, playing goalie for the Canadiens, Jacques Plante appeared against the Chicago Black Hawks in a Stanley Cup playoff game. "I don't believe I've ever been so nervous," Plante remembered later. "I couldn't even tie my skates." But in spite of his feelings, the rookie goaltender had a shutout in the first of his many NHL games—a fitting beginning for a long and sparkling career.

One of the first goaltenders to develop and use a "roaming" style of play, Plante often moved away from the immediate goal crease. He explained that he developed this method of play during his years as a goalie for some of the less skillful amateur teams. "I

Plante gets a ride on the shoulders of his teammates after he helped the Montreal Canadiens to the Stanley Cup in 1957.

(below) It's rough and tumble near the Montreal goal as Jacques Plante sends New York's Ron Murphy flying in the 1957 Stanley Cup playoffs.

was constantly having to chase the puck behind the net, and before long I realized that in this way—whether the team is bad or good—the goalie can often help himself," he said. The effectiveness of Plante's idea was soon noticed by other goalies, both professionals and amateurs, who copied his methods in their own play.

And there is no doubt that Jacques Plante's methods of goaltending were effective. In 10 campaigns with the Montreal Canadiens—from the 1953–54 season through the 1962–63 season—his play was the key to five straight Stanley Cup championships for the Canadiens. He was voted the league's All-Star netminder six times, and he was awarded the Vezina Trophy six times as well. And in 1962, Plante was given the Hart Trophy as the NHL's most valuable player. It was only the fourth time in NHL history that this award was won by a goalie.

During his 10 years with the Canadiens, Plante played at a record-setting pace. In six of those years, he led the NHL with the lowest average of goals scored against him. For five straight seasons from 1955–56 through 1959–60, Plante's goals-against averages were 1.86, 2.02, 2.11, 2.18, and 2.54. In the 1961–62 season, he again led the league with a 2.37 average. And for three straight seasons, 1956 through 1958, Plante also led the NHL in shutouts, with nine in each season.

At the end of the 1962–63 season, Plante had again led the league in shutouts with five and had a goals-against average of 2.49. Yet the Canadiens decided that the 34-year-old goalie might be reaching the end of his useful career. In a seven-man trade, Mon-

Plante, Jacques

Playing for the Blues, Plante kicks away a shot during the 1970 Stanley cup semifinal series with Pittsburgh.

treal sent Plante and two forwards, Donnie Marshall and Phil Goyette, to the New York Rangers. In return, the Canadiens got another noted goalie, Gump Worsley, and three forwards, Dave Balon, Leon Rochefort, and Len Ronson.

After two seasons of play for the Rangers—in which Plante's performance was not up to his old standards—the goaltender retired from hockey and became a salesman for a Canadian brewery. He left behind not only a fine record and a new style of play, but also a safety device—the plastic face mask.

Plante had been badly cut in the face in a game against the Rangers in 1959. He devised a plastic face mask for protection, and after his wound had been stitched up, he began to wear the mask regularly. The mask became not only his personal trademark but also a standard piece of equipment for nearly every goalie in hockey.

Making a Comeback

The offer of a fine salary and a return to the NHL in 1968 lured Plante out of retirement. He joined the St. Louis Blues, an expansion team. There, he alternated as goalie with Glenn Hall, another aging superstar. The Blues coach, Scotty Bowman, put Plante in 37 games. And the old pro posted the best goals-against average in the NHL for the seventh time—1.96.

In the playoffs in the 1968–69 season, Plante posted three shutouts in 10 games and had a goals-against average of 1.43.

Once again, in the 1969–70 season, Jacques Plante played well. Then, in May of 1970, he was traded to the Toronto Maple Leafs. Appearing in 40 games for the Leafs in the 1970–71 season, Plante again led the NHL with a 1.88 goals-against average.

Career Highlights

Led the Montreal Canadiens to six Stanley Cups (1953, 1956–60)

Won seven Vezina Trophies as the league's top goaltender

Named the NHL Most Valuable Player in 1962

Recorded 87 shutouts in his career

Became the first goalie to ever wear a mask

Elected to the Hockey Hall of Fame in 1979

"If you make a mistake, they turn on a red light behind you, a siren goes off and thousands of people scream."

—Jacques Plante, when describing the unique pressures faced by being a goaltender

Plante makes a neat glove save for St. Louis in 1969 against the Maple Leafs.

He also started in three playoff games. He stayed with the Leafs until midway through the 1972–73 season, when he was sold to the Boston Bruins.

The Bruins were desperate for a top-flight goalie to replace their regular man, Gerry Cheevers, who had moved to the World Hockey Association (WHA). The 44-year-old Plante proved to be the right man for them. He had two shutouts in eight games, and the Bruins finished second, behind only the Canadiens in the Eastern Division. Unfortunately, Plante's magic wore off in the playoffs that season as the Rangers eliminated the Bruins in the first round.

After the season ended, Plante signed a 10-year contract as head coach and general manager of the Quebec Nordiques of the WHA. His long and illustrious career as a goalie seemed to be over. But in 1974, he broke his contract with Quebec and joined the Edmonton Oilers of the WHA. He played one season before retiring permanently in 1975.

In 18 NHL seasons, Plante played in 838 games. Almost 10 percent of those games—82 of them—were shutouts. His career goals-against average was 2.38. In playoff games, Plante's record was even better. He compiled 15 shutouts and a goals-against average of 2.17 in 112 playoff contests. Elected to the Hockey Hall of Fame in 1978, Jacques Plante died of stomach cancer in Geneva, Switzerland, on February 26, 1986.

Further Study

BOOKS

Kramer, S.A. *Hockey's Greatest Players.* New York, NY: Random House, 1999.

WEB SITES

"Legends of Hockey," *Hockey Hall of Fame and Museum.* Online at www.legendsofhockey.net/html/legendsplayer.htm (November 2003)